RIVALS
★ UNTO ★
DEATH

Aaron Burr
(1756–1836)

Alexander Hamilton
(1755–1804)

RIVALS ★ UNTO ★ DEATH

Alexander Hamilton
and
Aaron Burr

RICK BEYER

New York Boston

Hachette Books
Hachette Book Group
1290 Avenue of the Americas
New York, NY 10104
hachettebookgroup.com
twitter.com/hachettebooks

First Edition: February 2017

Hachette Books is a division of Hachette Book Group, Inc.
The Hachette Books name and logo are trademarks of Hachette Book Group, Inc.

The publisher is not responsible for websites (or their content) that are not owned by the publisher.

The Hachette Speakers Bureau provides a wide range of authors for speaking events. To find out more, go to www.hachettespeakersbureau.com or call (866) 376-6591.

Aaron Burr image courtesy of the Library of Congress (LC-USZ62-52550).

Alexander Hamilton image courtesy of the Library of Congress (LC-D416-444).

Library of Congress Cataloging-in-Publication Data

Beyer, Rick, 1956- author.
Rivals Unto Death : Alexander Hamilton and Aaron Burr / Rick Beyer.
First edition. | New York : Hachette Books, 2017.
LCCN 2016047851| ISBN 9780316504973 (hardback) | ISBN 9781478917724
  (audio download) | ISBN 9780316504966 (ebook)
LCSH: Burr, Aaron, 1756-1836. | Hamilton, Alexander, 1757-1804. |
  Burr-Hamilton Duel, Weehawken, N.J., 1804. | BISAC: BIOGRAPHY &
  AUTOBIOGRAPHY / Presidents & Heads of State. | HISTORY / United States /
  Revolutionary Period (1775-1800).
LCC E302.6.H2 B49 2017 | DDC 973.4/6092—dc23 LC record available
at https://lccn.loc.gov/2016047851

ISBNs: 978-0-316-50497-3 (hardcover), 978-0-316-50496-6 (ebook).

Printed in the United States of America

LSC-C

10 9 8 7 6 5 4 3 2 1

For Marilyn,

who shares a birthday with Alexander Hamilton,
and shared in the creation of this book

CONTENTS

AUTHOR'S NOTE

I have taken the liberty of altering punctuation, abbreviations, spelling, and capitalization in some quotes to make them easier to read and understand.

The party founded by Thomas Jefferson in opposition to the Federalists was sometimes known as the Democratic party, sometimes the Republican party, and sometimes the Democratic-Republican party. For the sake of clarity I refer to it as the Republican party. It is not connected with today's Republican party, which was not founded until the 1850s.

To help readers keep track of the fascinating multitudes who parade through these pages, and to see what happened to them afterwards, there is a "Cast of Characters" section at the back of the book.

CHRONOLOGY

Hamilton's son Philip is born
Hamilton elected to Continental Congress

1783   Revolutionary War ends
British leave New York City after seven years of occupation
Burr and Hamilton set up law practices in New York

1784   Hamilton helps found Bank of New York
Burr elected to New York General Assembly

1786   Hamilton elected to New York General Assembly
Annapolis Commission meets

1787   Constitutional Convention
First of the Federalist Papers published

1788   New York Ratifying Convention

1789   Washington becomes president
Storming of the Bastille
Washington appoints Hamilton secretary of the treasury
New York Governor George Clinton appoints Burr state attorney general

1790   Dinner table bargain between Hamilton, Thomas Jefferson, and James Madison
Capital moves to Philadelphia

1791   Burr defeats Philip Schuyler in race for U.S. senator from New York
Hamilton begins affair with Maria Reynolds

1792   Burr runs for governor of New York, eventually withdraws
Burr runs for vice president, Hamilton secretly attacks him

1793   French King Louis XVI guillotined

France declares war on England, United States declares neutrality

Citizen Genêt tours United States

1794 Burr's wife Theodosia dies

Washington and Hamilton lead army to put down Whiskey Rebellion

1795 Hamilton resigns from Treasury

Jay Treaty made public, generating fierce controversy

1796 Burr runs again for governor of New York, eventually withdraws

Burr defeated in second run for vice president

John Adams elected president, Jefferson elected vice president

1797 Burr loses U.S. Senate seat

Hamilton confronts Madison, Burr helps avert duel

Hamilton publishes Reynolds Pamphlet detailing affair

XYZ Affair

1798 Quasi-War with France

Burr elected to New York General Assembly

Hamilton appointed deputy commander of the provisional army

Washington declines to appoint Burr as army quartermaster

Congress passes Alien and Sedition Acts

1799 Washington dies

Burr forms Manhattan Company, which went on to become Chase Manhattan Bank, now JPMorgan Chase Bank

Burr duels John Barker Church (no one hurt)

1800 Hamilton and Burr defend Levi Weeks in murder trial
Burr engineers critical victory in New York legislative elections
Jefferson and Burr tie in run for president
Capital moves to Washington, D.C.

1801 House of Representatives elects Jefferson president on 36th ballot
Hamilton's son Philip killed in duel
Hamilton founds *New York Post*

1802 Pamphlet Wars begin

1804 Burr defeated in New York gubernatorial election
Burr challenges Hamilton to duel and kills him

1805 Burr journeys west to mount a controversial military expedition

1807 Burr tried for treason, acquitted

1813 Burr's daughter Theodosia dies in shipwreck

1836 Burr dies

1854 Eliza Hamilton dies

1929 Hamilton pictured on $10 bill

TEN

FACE-TO-FACE

One week before

On July Fourth, 1804, a boisterous Independence Day celebration took place at Fraunces Tavern, the convivial New York City watering hole where George Washington had bid an emotional farewell to his officers in 1783. Already nearly a century old, the brick building on the corner of Pearl and Broad had housed a tavern since before the Revolution, and was one of the most popular gathering spots in the city. Approximately seventy-five men crammed in around narrow wooden tables that ran the length of the tavern's Long Room. There were lawyers and bankers, merchants and gentleman farmers. They all had one thing in common: in their youth, they had served as comrades-in-arms in the war that transformed their lives and gave birth to the new nation.

The occasion was the gala annual banquet of the Society of the Cincinnati, the organization founded by officers who had served in Washington's army. The tables were soon cluttered with dishes bearing a sumptuous feast. Wine and rum punch flowed freely. No sooner were the dishes cleared away than the diners launched into a series of formal toasts. By tradition there were seventeen, one for each state. This was a night to let loose, an evening of "harmony and social glee," according to the society's minutes. Songs, jests, and shouts filled the air, and smoke from a dozen clay pipes curled toward the low ceiling as they celebrated the country's twenty-eighth birthday.

Seated side by side in places of honor at one of the long tables were two men who served on Washington's staff during the war, and whose destinies had been intertwined ever since: Alexander Hamilton and Aaron Burr.

The drink-fueled revelry went on late into the night, but the flickering candlelight that played upon Burr and Hamilton showed a marked contrast in their demeanors. "The singularity of their manner was observed by all," commented artist John Trumbull, who was a special guest at the event. "Burr, contrary to his wont, was silent, gloomy, sour; while Hamilton entered with glee into all the gaiety of a convivial party, and even sung an old military song."

According to one account, the song Hamilton chose to sing for the assembled gathering was "How Stands the Glass Around." It was popularly known as "Wolfe's Song," because legend had it that British General James Wolfe sang the song the night before his great victory in the Battle of Quebec in 1759—a victory that cost him his life. A boisterous drinking song filled with spirited bravado, it possessed a certain poignant irony because of its connection with Wolfe's heroic death.

> Why, soldiers, why?
> Should we be melancholy, boys?
> Why, soldiers, why?
> Whose business is to die!

As Hamilton sang, Burr raised his head and gazed intently at him, seemingly lost in thought.

They had much in common, these two. Both were orphans, Revolutionary War heroes, lawyers, and politicians. In addition, they were two of the most well-known men in America. Burr, after all, was the sitting vice president, under Thomas Jefferson, just a heartbeat away from the presidency. Hamilton had served President Washington as the nation's first secretary of the treasury, creating out of whole cloth the systems that formed the underpinnings of the nation's economy. They were longtime rivals in the cockpit of New York politics, where they had sometimes worked together, but far more often battled each other with increasing loathing. Once they had been friends, but no shred of that friendship survived.

At any point in the evening, did a look pass between them? A grimace, a glare, a half smile? A clue to their innermost thoughts? The revelers celebrating around them had no way of knowing that the two men shared a dark secret, one they kept well hidden that night. Their differences had reached the point of no return, and they had come to the mutual conclusion that there was only one way to settle them:

In a duel, with pistols, in one week's time.

Seven days later, Aaron Burr woke up on his couch as dawn broke over Richmond Hill, his New York City mansion. He had slept in his clothes, over which he now put on an elegant black frock coat made of silk. It was a deliciously cool morning for July. The grounds of his house sloped down to the Hudson River, and it took him less than a minute to walk to the water's edge. He was with a friend, William Van Ness, who was acting as his second—his representative in making arrangements for the duel. They were met by a small boat and rowed across the mile-wide Hudson by a single oarsman.

Their destination was a small beach at the base of the cliffs in Weehawken, New Jersey. From there, a narrow path led up to a rocky ledge about twenty feet above the water, opening onto a clearing about the size of a volleyball court. It was a secluded spot, surrounded by dense woods and heavy undergrowth. No trail led down from the heights, two hundred feet above. No houses were in view on that side of the river. In other words, it was a perfect spot for a duel, and a number of them had been fought there. Dueling was illegal in both New York and New Jersey, but New York was more aggressive about prosecuting duelists, so those determined to shoot it out often headed across the water.

The site offered a spectacular view across the Hudson, for anyone who took the time to notice. Far off to the right, barely visible in the morning haze, was Staten Island. Then New York City, still only covering the tip of Manhattan, its waterfront surrounded by a forest of ships' masts. Woods and occasional farms stretched north of the city into the distance, covering most of the rest of Manhattan.

Burr and Van Ness stepped out of the boat and climbed up a few dozen steps to the ledge. They took off their frock coats and began clearing away accumulated brush to prepare for the encounter, which would follow the carefully prescribed rules of the *Code Duello*. This detailed set of dueling instructions had been drawn up in Ireland in the 1770s, after pistols had become the preferred weapon for dueling. Its provisions were well known to gentlemen in Europe and America.

Alexander Hamilton set out across the Hudson from a separate dock some time after Burr. He was accompanied by a slightly larger entourage that included his second, Judge Nathaniel Pendleton; his doctor, David Hosack; and two oarsmen. Since Burr was the challenger, Hamilton had the choice of weapons. Sitting at his feet in the boat was a wooden chest containing two ornate flintlock pistols, with lacquered walnut handles and brass barrels. The guns held a tragic memory for Hamilton, one that he undoubtedly reflected upon in the hour or so that it took to cross the broad expanse of the Hudson.

Hamilton arrived on the Jersey side of the river at about 7 A.M. He walked up to the ledge with Pendleton, while the oarsmen and the doctor remained at the boat to maintain plausible deniability in the event of a trial. Hamilton and Burr offered each other a strained greeting, while Pendleton and Van Ness made the final arrangements for the showdown. They measured the distance that would separate the two duelists—ten paces. Then they cast lots to see who would have choice of position, and whose second would give the final word—the winner was Hamilton on both counts. There was no talk of a last-minute apology to avert the duel. After years of mutual antagonism, neither man had the slightest interest in backing down now.

Burr and Hamilton took their stations. Hamilton, given the choice of position, selected the northernmost spot. It was an odd choice; the way the ledge faced the river put the rising summer sun in his eyes. The two seconds handed fully loaded and cocked pistols to the principals. The two-pound Wogdon dueling pistols were of a large caliber, capable of eviscerating an opponent at this range. Pendleton then explained the rules. He would ask if both men were ready. When they were, he would shout the word "Present!" After that, they could fire when they pleased.

Pendleton asked if both men were set. Burr's gaze was fixed on

Hamilton. "He caught my eye, and quailed under it," Burr later commented. "He looked like a convicted felon." Hamilton did seem unnerved by the moment. "Stop," he called out. Heads turned quizzically toward him, looking for an explanation. "In certain states of the light," Hamilton explained, "one requires glasses."

As Burr watched with silent disdain, Hamilton aimed his pistol at imaginary targets in various directions, squinting in the light. Then he put on his glasses, and repeated the ritual. Finally, he decided he would wear his glasses for the duel. "This will do now," he said. "You may proceed."

Burr and Hamilton stood like statues, each holding his pistol at the ready. A light breeze rustled through the tree branches.

"Present!" shouted Pendleton.

The two seconds differed about what happened next, but they both agreed on one point. "Both parties took aim..."

It is the most famous duel in American history. Two of the nation's founders, shooting it out with pistols, within sight of New York City. But exactly why were they there? What so inflamed these two men, on this day, that they could think of no better way to resolve the issues between them?

Hamilton was a Federalist, a fervent supporter of a powerful central government as a check against the passions of the mob. Burr was affiliated with Jefferson's Republican party, which feared placing too much power in the hands of the elite. (The conflict over this issue remains intense two-hundred-plus years later.) Their duel came at a time when the country was young and vulnerable. A real fear that political disagreements might literally tear the country apart was never far from the surface. Politics alone, though, only goes so far in explaining the animosity between these two.

Hamilton's pugnacious personality is often cited as a factor. He reduced many leading luminaries of the day to spluttering anger with his abrasive attacks, while himself being hypersensitive to the slightest perceived slight. This combination of qualities involved him in as many as ten "affairs of honor" over the years. Yet all except this one were settled long before they reached the dueling ground.

History and popular culture have generally put the blame on Burr, making him the undisputed villain in this drama. He laid down the challenge, he fired the bullet that killed Hamilton, and he was later tried for treason. He must be the bad guy, the argument goes. End of story. Such a conclusion can only be reached by ignoring the complexities of Burr's character, and in any case fails to unravel the many strands of this convoluted melodrama that was carried out on the national stage.

The Hamilton-Burr story is a murder mystery where the *who* is beyond doubt, but the *why* is endlessly fascinating. To search for clues, we must spin the story backwards, past the exchange of acrimonious notes that led to the duel, past the tumultuous 1800 election that turned on Hamilton and Burr's private war, further and further, before the sex scandal that so damaged Hamilton's career, and the other duels that litter this story, past friends and enemies such as Thomas Jefferson, James Madison, and John Adams, not the myths, but the flesh-and-blood men, traveling back to a time before the first outbreak of partisan politics came in response to the Constitution that Hamilton so fervently espoused, and Burr coolly opposed, rewinding past the days when they were friends and colleagues, through the New York courtrooms where they both argued, back before they were law students, all the way back to the very first days of the American Revolution. The roots of their rivalry can be discerned in the complicated relationship each of them had with the august figure whose exploits were toasted at Fraunces Tavern one week before the duel: George Washington.

NINE

FIRST SHOT

Twenty-nine years before

The first shot of the American Revolution was fired a few minutes before dawn, on April 19, 1775. British soldiers decked out in scarlet and drawn up in tight formation faced two ragged lines of colonial militiamen on the town common in Lexington, Massachusetts. A musket barked. A skirmish broke out. That led to a battle at the North Bridge in Concord, and then a brawling, bloody, running gunfight between retreating British regulars and angry colonial militiamen all the way back to the British lines in Boston. By nightfall, forty-nine colonials and seventy-three British soldiers had been killed. More than three thousand militiamen camped on the outskirts of Boston, penning the British inside the city. They were farmers, millers, wheelwrights, men of every description who had taken up arms to fight British tyranny. The War for Independence was now a fact. In the coming days and weeks, thousands more volunteers flooded into the camps from nearby colonies. By early June it became clear to the Continental Congress, meeting in Philadelphia, that this growing army needed a commander. They chose a tall Virginia planter who had served as a colonel in the French and Indian War, and whose stern self-control hid a storm of emotions raging just beneath the surface.

George Washington hurried north from Philadelphia to take up his new command. On June 25, cheering crowds lined Broadway as Washington rode through New York City in a majestic carriage drawn by four white horses. A company of militiamen marched alongside as an honor guard. Among the throngs of people cheering him on was an ambitious twenty-year-old who had arrived from the West Indies not long before. Alexander Hamilton was already making a name for himself, but he could hardly guess that within two years he would be one of Washington's closest aides.

Hamilton was born in 1755[1] on the remote Caribbean island of Nevis, situated east of Puerto Rico, nearly two thousand miles from New York. He was the illegitimate son of James Hamilton and Rachel Faucette. John Adams, who was to become a bitter enemy of Alexander Hamilton, accurately but uncharitably referred to him as "the bastard brat of a Scotch peddler." Hamilton was understandably circumspect about his early years. His father, the fourth son of a Scottish lord, came to the Caribbean to seek his fortune, but failed miserably as a merchant. His mother had fled an abusive husband on the island of St. Croix without ever getting divorced. James and Rachel had two sons out of wedlock before James abandoned his family.

Rachel moved back to St. Croix in 1765 with the two boys. She died three years later, leaving her sons as orphans.

---

1. There is some question as to whether Hamilton was born in 1755 or 1757. Recent scholarship inclines toward the earlier date, which is what is used here.

Things went from bad to worse. Alexander Hamilton and his older brother were adopted by a cousin who committed suicide shortly afterward. Rachel's first husband seized her estate, leaving the boys with virtually nothing. At this point, their lives diverged. James became apprenticed to a local carpenter. Little is known of his later life, spent entirely in the Virgin Islands; he died sometime after 1785.

At age thirteen, Alex began working as a clerk in a mercantile firm. Soon he was sending out commanding missives to ship captains and traders, acting with maturity far beyond his years. Shortly afterwards he was adopted by a family friend, Thomas Stevens. Hamilton was only fourteen when he wrote to his adopted brother Ned Stevens that he could not bear to think about "groveling forever as a clerk" because "my ambition is prevalent." A poor orphan boy stuck on an obscure island, he nonetheless had his sights set high, and would "willingly risk my life, though not my character, to exalt my station." At the end of the letter he expressed a striking sentiment. "I wish there was a war." A war, he thought, might provide enough upheaval to take him away from the islands and give him a chance to show what he was capable of.

It was not a war, however, but a hurricane that blew Hamilton out of the West Indies. After the destructive storm tore through St. Croix in August 1772, Hamilton wrote a vivid letter describing the damage and reflecting upon its impact. "The roaring of the sea and wind, fiery meteors flying about it in the air, the prodigious glare of almost perpetual lightning, the crash of the falling houses, and the ear-piercing shrieks of the distressed, were sufficient to strike astonishment into Angels." The letter was published in a local newspaper, both its prose and religious fervor impressing many. A minister took up a collection to send this prodigiously talented young man off to school in New York City. There he attended King's College (renamed Columbia College after the Revolution[2]), and started studying law. In 1774, when the nineteen-year-old Hamilton gave a rousing speech at a mass rally for the Sons of Liberty, it turned heads. After the battles of Lexington and Concord, Hamilton joined a local militia company and began boning up on military strategy, while writing fiery pamphlets in defense of the patriot cause. Slight in stature with piercing blue eyes and red hair, he was already a manic overachiever, brimming with energy and restless impatience. Whatever the future held, he would make the most of it.

George Washington arrived in Cambridge, Massachusetts, on July 2, 1775, to take command of the Continental Army. Only two weeks before, the colonials had been roundly defeated at the Battle of Bunker Hill. Washington's job was to mold this motley collection of barely trained and poorly equipped citizen-soldiers into an army. He set up his headquarters at a stately mansion in Cambridge that later became the home of the poet Henry Wadsworth Longfellow. In early August, two young gentlemen from "The Jerseys" presented themselves to Washington bearing a letter of introduction from none other than John Hancock, president of the Continental Congress. The letter said they were visiting Washington's camp "not as spectators, but with a view of joining the army and being active during the campaign." One was named Matthias Ogden. The other was a well-connected nineteen-year-old with a distinguished bloodline named Aaron Burr.

---

2. Now Columbia University.

Burr's maternal grandfather was the famous preacher and theologian Jonathan Edwards. His father, also named Aaron Burr, was the president of what would become Princeton University. Both his parents died when he was an infant, and he was raised by his uncle. Burr graduated from Princeton at sixteen, giving a senior oration in which he cautioned his fellow students against wasting their time on dreams and far-fetched schemes. Standing five feet six, with hazel eyes and a gentlemanly bearing, he was known affectionately to his classmates as "Little Burr." He considered following in his grandfather's footsteps as a minister, but eventually decided on a legal career. He had just begun his studies when the war broke out.

Washington was not ready to offer commissions to Burr and his friend Ogden, but he let them hang around as volunteers. Despite having come down with a fever, Burr volunteered to join an expedition being led by Benedict Arnold to seize Quebec City, a British stronghold. Later to become famous for treason and treachery, the headstrong Arnold was already a war hero for his role in helping to capture Fort Ticonderoga. He led a force of 1,100 men north to Canada, intending to link up with another army under General Richard Montgomery, and capture Quebec.

It was a brutal six-hundred-mile journey, much of it through unforgiving wilderness. Food ran low and hunger took its toll, as did the oncoming winter. Conditions were so miserable that three companies of volunteers simply turned back. Ogden feared that Burr, still weak from his debilitating bout with fever, wouldn't survive. Yet the slender young man seemed to thrive under the hardships. He wrote a jaunty letter to his sister describing what he considered to be his outlandish outfit: a fringe jacket, a hat with a foxtail attached (to make him look taller, he joked), along with a musket, bayonet, and toma-hawk. In a nod to the harsh conditions that prevailed, he told her that the one item he never let out of his sight was his blanket.

By mid-November, death and desertion had reduced Arnold's force to 675 men, many of whom were on the verge of starvation. He made camp twenty miles from Quebec and sent Burr to find General Mont-gomery's force. The message from Arnold praised the messenger as "a young man of much life and activity who has acted with great spirit and resolution on our fatiguing march." Montgomery was impressed with young Burr, and appointed him to a position as a captain on his staff. Handsome, dashing, and with a flair for command, Montgom-ery seemed the romantic ideal of a general. He made a great impres-sion on Burr, who quickly became an admirer.

Even for the combined forces of Montgomery and Arnold, Quebec would be a tough nut to crack. It was a fortress city on a high hill, with walls rising all around. To make matters worse, the two Ameri-can generals did not have time on their side. They needed to attack quickly, as many of their men's enlistments would run out on Janu-ary 1, 1776. They planned a desperate New Year's Eve assault. Under the cover of snow, each general would lead a column through the lower city, outside the walls, then link up for assault on the citadel that loomed overhead.

Instead of a gentle snow, however, Montgomery and his men faced a raging blizzard that slowed them down as they approached the dark-ened city. Everything looked deserted. Surprise seemed to be on their side. "We shall be in the fort in two minutes," said Montgomery. At just that moment, Canadian militiamen concealed in a fortified build-ing opened fire. Montgomery and two aides were mortally wounded.

His second-in-command ordered the men to retreat. Burr and two others stayed behind to cover the movement. As musket fire rained down on them, Burr tried to carry the general's body back, but was unable to do so. The attack fell apart. The column under General Arnold fared no better. Fifty colonials were killed, and hundreds captured. Arnold withdrew his forces outside the city walls, but continued to besiege Quebec with the remnants of his army.

In the aftermath of the battle, Burr described himself as "dirty, ragged, moneyless and friendless." His hero, Montgomery, was dead. His friend Ogden, wounded in the fighting, had gone home to recuperate. War had lost some of its luster. Congress, he raged, must have been "drunk or crazy" to send such a small force to capture Quebec. At the same time, Burr was also aware that his own reputation was on the rise. He had acted with great bravery under fire, and people were taking notice. A friend in Philadelphia later wrote to him, "Tis said you behaved well...The gentlemen of Congress speak highly of you." Burr was too proud to actively seek promotion, but felt his performance had earned it, and he waited impatiently for others to see it the same way.

Alexander Hamilton, in the meantime, was also advancing. Before the war, he had caught the attention of patriot leader Alexander McDougall, a fiery Scot who had spent years as a sea captain before prospering as a New York merchant. Now a colonel in the Continental Army, McDougall saw to it that Hamilton was appointed captain of an artillery company. Hamilton was thrilled with his new position. He went to work training his men and laying out a fortified position on Bayard's Hill in Manhattan. The young man from the Caribbean was filled with patriotic fervor for his adopted country. "I was born to die and my reason and conscience tell me it is impossible to die in a better or more important cause." Once upon a time he had wished for a war. Now the war was coming to him.

The Battle of New York was the biggest clash of the Revolution. Because it was such a disaster for the Americans, it is also one of the least remembered. The British invasion fleet that sailed into New York Harbor in the summer of 1776 contained more than four hundred ships and transports carrying thirty-five thousand soldiers and sailors, the biggest British expeditionary force until World War I. Facing them was an army of twenty-five thousand men serving under an untested general, George Washington, who had never led an army into battle before.

From August until November of 1776, these two forces clashed in a series of engagements that ranged across Brooklyn, up the streets of Manhattan, into Harlem and Westchester, and finally across to New Jersey. The colonials suffered a crushing defeat. Washington lost more than three-quarters of his army. And on one critical day in September, Alexander Hamilton and Aaron Burr would find themselves in the same small corner of the war.

That spring Burr was still despondent, and harbored bitter thoughts that his friends had abandoned him in their own quests for advancement. His mood improved noticeably when Matthias Ogden, already promoted to lieutenant colonel, procured for Burr an appointment to the staff of General Washington. Here was a glittering opportunity, a chance to work directly for the man leading the fight for independence. Burr arrived in New York a few weeks before the British, in early June 1776. He joined Washington as he was preparing for the

British onslaught. Washington's headquarters was in the Richmond Hill mansion that would later become Burr's own home.

The young hero of Quebec, however, felt anything but comfortable. He left Washington's staff after only ten days, trading places with an aide to General Israel Putnam. As a combat veteran, Burr may have chafed at the duties of a lowly staffer to a great man, copying letters and running errands. With a battle looming, he may have yearned for a position closer to the action. It seems likely, however, that there was something more to his departure. His longtime friend Matthew Livingston Davis, who became his first biographer, wrote, "his prejudices against General Washington were immoveable. They were formed in the summer of 1776, while he resided at the headquarters."

Perhaps the austere Washington failed to live up to the example Montgomery set of how a dashing general should act. Or maybe Burr felt Washington did not treat him with the respect due his experience on the battlefield. There may have been some sort of incident that turned Washington against Burr. In any event, what's clear is that Burr's decision to remove himself from Washington's orbit was a pivotal one. The man who replaced him, Major Samuel Webb, soon became part of Washington's inner circle. He rose to the rank of brigadier general, and officiated as grand marshal at Washington's presidential inauguration in 1789. That could have been Aaron Burr. He chose a different path.

A week after Burr left Washington's staff, the British armada moved into New York Bay. Down in Philadelphia, Thomas Jefferson was putting the finishing touches on a document that would declare the colonies "free and independent states," but the overwhelming British invasion force raised doubts that the Declaration of Independence would mean very much in the long run. General William Howe began the Battle of New York on August 22, landing fifteen thousand troops on Long Island, including German mercenaries known as Hessians. Washington's corps was no match for them, and soon the general withdrew to Manhattan. He placed most of his troops north of the city, in what is now Harlem, but stationed five thousand men in lower Manhattan under the command of General Israel Putnam. This force included Alexander Hamilton and Aaron Burr.

On September 15, Howe launched his attack on Manhattan. British troops sailed up the East River and landed at Kips Bay, near what is now 34th Street. Five British warships launched broadside after broadside against American fortifications as the landing craft hit the beaches. Their eighty cannons provided "so terrible and so incessant a roar of guns few even in the Army and Navy had ever heard before," wrote one British observer. The American militia manning the defenses fled.

Washington, who had expected the attack to take place up in Harlem, raced down on horseback to stem the retreat. He tried to rally his men in a cornfield north of where the 42nd Street New York Public Library stands today. Despite his efforts, the appearance of a small British contingent prompted the militia to turn and run up Bloomingdale Road, as the northern portion of Broadway was then called. From his horse, an enraged Washington lashed out with his cane at fleeing officers, to no avail. He flung his hat to the ground in disgust. "Good God!" he exclaimed. "Have I got such troops as these?"

General Israel Putnam's troops in lower Manhattan were now at risk of being trapped, so Washington ordered Putnam to withdraw.

Aaron Burr had settled in as an aide to Putnam, whom he called his "good old general." He helped Putnam pull off the daring retreat in the face of the attacking British force. He knew the city better than his chief, and helped guide the troops to safety. In doing so, he may well have saved Alexander Hamilton's life.

By late afternoon, virtually all of the American troops had abandoned Manhattan except for the men at Bayard's Hill, a rough-hewn fort south of present-day Chinatown. The commander there, Colonel Gold Silliman, apparently had not received word to retreat. When Burr discovered that Silliman's men were still manning the fort, he pleaded with the colonel to withdraw before he was surrounded. Silliman was stubbornly determined to fight it out "to the last man."

According to Burr's own account, he devised a clever ruse to convince the colonel. He rode off, waited a few minutes, and rode back, saying he now brought orders from General Putnam demanding that Silliman withdraw. As he led the men north, they ran into an advance guard of the enemy. Burr and several other horsemen rode directly at them, killing a few and driving off the rest. Galloping back, he discovered that Silliman's men had taken a wrong turn. He led them through a woods to get back on the right road, and eventually reunited them with Washington's troops in Harlem.

Hamilton's artillery company was among those stationed at Bayard's Hill, and Hamilton later wrote, "I was among the last of our army that left the city." It seems almost certain that he was among the men that Burr led to safety, although neither man ever made mention of that fact. Had Burr not convinced Silliman to retreat, Hamilton's fate would most likely have been grim. Many Americans captured during the Battle of New York perished amid squalid conditions on British prison ships. As it was, Hamilton and his men managed to

bring two of the artillery pieces with them as they retreated up the
island, although Hamilton lost all of his personal baggage. The British settled down to occupy New York, and it would be seven years
before either Burr or Hamilton made it back to the city.

Two of the soldiers involved in the retreat that afternoon remembered that Burr's "coolness, deliberation, and valor" gained him
"respect from the troops, and the particular notice of the officers."
By some accounts, his feat was the talk of the army. Burr thought
he deserved a commendation from General Washington. When none
was forthcoming, Burr seethed at what he felt was an injustice done to
him by the commander-in-chief.

Washington's army, a mere shadow of what it had been, retreated
into New Jersey. On Christmas night, Washington famously led his
men in a bold crossing of the Delaware River and a surprise attack
on the hated Hessian troops in Trenton. It was a tiny battle, involving one-tenth of the men who had fought in the Battle of New York,
but the victory proved a shot in the arm for colonial morale. In future
years, it became a point of honor to have been one of the "band of
brothers" that fought at Trenton. Burr and Hamilton were both
there, as were two future presidents, James Madison and James Monroe, and a future chief justice of the Supreme Court, John Marshall.

Hamilton had come down with a fever, but he rose from his sick-
bed to take part in the battle, firing his cannon on the Hessians to
help force their surrender. People were beginning to take notice of
the red-haired artillery captain, described by one observer around
this time as "a youth, a mere stripling, small, slender, almost delicate
in frame." One of those who liked what he saw in the diminutive

officer was General Washington, who made Hamilton a lieutenant colonel and appointed him to his staff.

Hamilton would go on to serve the general for four years. He became Washington's most important aide and his lifelong protégé. Washington relied heavily on his staff: "It is absolutely necessary... for me to have persons that can think for me as well as execute orders." In young Hamilton he found someone with prodigious energy, a head bursting with ideas, and a passionate desire to prove himself. Although Washington had half a dozen young officers on his staff, Hamilton quickly became his "principal and most confidential aide," as Washington himself put it.

Even at this early age, Hamilton showed a bottomless capacity for hard work. Like many other immigrants, he may have felt that he had to work twice as hard as everyone else to prove himself. A prolific and powerful writer, Hamilton drafted letters to congressmen, governors, and generals. He wrote out many of Washington's field orders. Hamilton sorted through intelligence, interrogated prisoners, negotiated prisoner exchanges, and conducted sensitive missions for the general. An older aide bestowed on him the affectionate nickname the "Little Lion." Once France came into the war on the American side, the bilingual Hamilton became invaluable as a translator and liaison. General Nathanael Greene remembered his presence at HQ as "a bright gleam of sunshine, ever growing brighter as the general darkness thickened."

Hamilton was not the only one rewarded for his conduct in battle. At long last, Aaron Burr's courage, daring, and fortitude drew notice from the commanding general. If Washington had been ill disposed toward Burr, he had clearly moved past it. In June 1777, he made Burr a lieutenant colonel and attached him as second-in-command to a regiment that had been raised by a wealthy New York merchant named William Malcolm. Since Malcolm did not spend much time with the regiment, Burr would be its de facto commander much of the time. It was the field command that Burr had long desired. Surprisingly, his response to it was anything but positive.

Instead of thanking Washington for the command, Burr complained that his promotion had taken too long, thus making him subordinate to officers promoted before him. "I am nevertheless, sir, constrained to observe that the late date of my appointment subjects me to the command of many who are younger in the service and junior officers in the last campaign." Then, in words dripping with icy disdain, Burr questioned Washington's motives. "I would beg to know, whether it was any misconduct in me or extraordinary merit or services in them, which entitled the gentlemen lately put over me, to that preference." Burr contended he had been deprived of the rank that he deserved because of his diligence and attention to duty.

Many officers in the Continental Army were sensitive about issues of rank, but young Burr's caustic tone, clearly communicating his cold fury, must have rankled the commanding general. Washington aide Tench Tilghman scrawled a single word on the bottom of it. "Unanswered." The letter almost certainly soured whatever positive opinion Washington was beginning to form about Burr.

The British Army marched on Philadelphia. "Congress was chased like a covey of partridges," wrote John Adams, a delegate from Massachusetts who had led the fight for independence that summer. The British took up residence in the city, and Washington's army spent the winter of 1777–1778 at Valley Forge, Pennsylvania, about twenty miles northwest of the city. The descriptions of the hardships they endured have become a staple of American history books. The snow was stained with blood from the soldiers' bare feet. Hunger, disease, and misery became the lot of Washington's men. Two thousand five hundred of Washington's men perished that winter. Burr struggled to keep discipline among the Malcolms, as his unit was known. He was not alone. "I know not how we shall keep the army together or make another campaign," wrote Hamilton.

Hamilton was burning the candle at both ends, staying up late at night to read about philosophy, history, and economics. He filled up a notebook with 112 pages of notes. He was beginning to develop a political philosophy that would guide him for his entire life. The young aide could see firsthand the ways in which Washington's army suffered because the government did not have the power to levy taxes to finance the war or secure adequate supplies to carry it through. Washington was constantly pleading with the Continental Congress for help. Typical was a letter he wrote in 1780: "It is with infinite pain that I inform Congress that we are reduced again to a situation of extremity for a want of meat." The root of the problem, as Hamilton saw it, was that the Articles of Confederation, under which the Continental Congress operated, did not grant it enough power. "The confederation itself is defective and requires to be altered; it is neither fit for war, nor peace." His solution? A powerful central government, led by a strong executive. When a single man was in charge, he wrote, "There is always more decision, more dispatch, more secrecy, more responsibility."

Hamilton formed close friendships with two other young officers serving Washington. One was John Laurens, whose father was a South Carolina plantation owner and a member of the Continental Congress. The other was a French officer who had outfitted a ship at his own expense to come to America and serve General Washington.

His full name was Marie-Joseph Paul Yves Roch Gilbert du Motier, but he is better known to history as the Marquis de Lafayette. The three were inseparable. Lafayette later called Hamilton "my beloved friend in whose brotherly affection I felt equally proud and happy." They would all be involved in an incident that would find Hamilton and Burr drawing opposite conclusions about the actions of General Washington.

In June 1778, the British withdrew their army from Philadelphia back to New York. General Henry Clinton stopped his ten thousand men for the night in the town of Monmouth Courthouse, New Jersey. Washington called a council of his officers. Some thought he should simply let the British go, but Washington overruled them and decided to attack with his advance guard and follow up with the rest of his army.

The man Washington wanted to lead the attack was the person most strongly opposed to it. General Charles Lee, Washington's second-in-command, was an eccentric, slovenly, temperamental officer who believed he should be in command instead of Washington. His verdict on the Virginian: "Not fit to command a sergeant's guard." Lee had served in the British Army before coming to the colonies, and had far more experience as a battlefield commander than Washington. Captured by the British in 1776, he had recently been exchanged after fifteen months of imprisonment. Hamilton was among those who questioned his loyalty, both to Washington and to the patriot cause.

Lee argued that it was foolhardy to attack the British, that colonial troops couldn't stand up to British bayonets. Lee was reluctant to lead the charge, but when Washington threatened to assign Lafayette instead, Lee grudgingly went along. Washington's orders stipulated that Lee should attack "unless there should be very powerful reasons to the contrary."

June 28, 1778, was a scorcher. The temperature rose well into the nineties. Scores of soldiers on both sides that day dropped because of the suffocating heat, and many stripped off their clothes to fight bare-chested. Lee was supposed to attack the rear of the British column early in the morning, as it moved out of Monmouth Courthouse. Despite exhortations from Lafayette, he was hesitant to move against them. After some confused maneuvering and skirmishing, the British brought up more forces to face the attacking Americans. Fighting had barely begun when Lee ordered his troops to retreat.

Washington, bringing up the rest of the army, was shocked to find his advance guard making a pell-mell dash for the rear. Hamilton, who had been at the front, galloped up to Washington, leaped off his horse, and ran to his commander. "General! We are betrayed! General Lee has betrayed you and the army." Washington's fury overwhelmed him. By the time he reached Lee, Major Jacob Morton said Washington "looked like a thunder cloud before the lightning flash."

"My God, Lee, what are you about?" Washington demanded. "I desire to know, sir, what is the reason for this disorder and confusion."

Lee stammered to explain his actions, but Washington would have none of it. The general, who normally strived to display self-control, exploded in anger. Lafayette, who was there, heard him call Lee "a damned poltroon"—a coward. Another officer said Washington cursed Lee "until the leaves shook on the trees." Washington eventually ordered Lee to the rear and undertook to rally the troops himself.

The Battle of Monmouth proved to be one of Washington's finest hours. Riding his white charger, he personally led the troops in renewing the attack on the enemy. Soldiers dropped from exhaustion in the soaring temperatures, but Washington refused give up. He seemed to be everywhere on the battlefield. Under his leadership, the army staved off defeat and fought to a draw. The battle ended in mutual exhaustion. Lafayette was overcome with admiration, saying, "Never had I beheld so superb a man." Said Hamilton, "His coolness and firmness were admirable...by his own good sense and fortitude he turned the fate of the day."

Hamilton worked himself into a frenzy on the battlefield. He seemed to court death as he rode to and fro. As Washington was giving orders to General Lee, Hamilton exclaimed, "Let us all die rather than retreat!" In the fighting that followed, Hamilton's horse was shot out from under him. Exhausted by the heat and injured by the fall, he had to be helped from the field.

Aaron Burr also had his horse shot out from under him at Monmouth. Burr was leading the Malcolms on the left wing. Finding himself in the thick of the action, he saw an opportunity to take on an isolated group of redcoats. He was held back when one of Washington's aides ordered him to stay in place. Burr's second-in-command was killed by a cannonball, and he himself was overcome by crippling heatstroke accompanied by severe nausea. He was laid low with migraine headaches, eye trouble, and depression. He told friends he was desperate to spend some time "remote from the noise of war." Doctors today might diagnose him as suffering from post-traumatic stress disorder (PTSD).

The day after the battle, General Lee wrote to Washington complaining about "the singular expressions" Washington used on the battlefield. He believed that in withdrawing when he did, he had saved the advance guard from destruction. He suggested that Washington's anger must have been "instigated by some of those dirty earwigs who will forever insinuate themselves near persons in high office," likely meaning Hamilton, Laurens, and Lafayette. Lee was eventually court-martialed for disobeying orders, fleeing the enemy, and showing disrespect for his superior. He was convicted on all charges.

Hamilton thought Lee's behavior "monstrous and impardonable" and testified against him at the court-martial. Burr thought Lee was being scapegoated for Washington's blunders, and wrote him a warm letter of support. When Lee eventually went public with his criticism of Washington, Hamilton's close friend John Laurens challenged him to a duel. Hamilton agreed to be Laurens's second.

This was the first of many "affairs of honor" that Hamilton would be involved with over his lifetime. The practice of dueling was hundreds of years old, and it would continue in the United States up to the time of the Civil War. Duels were not necessarily fought with the idea of killing your opponent, but demonstrating your willingness to die in defense of your honor. Often a simple exchange of shots was enough. When the participants' blood was up, however, duels could quickly become murderous affairs.

During the Revolution, there was a great deal of dueling in the army over matters of honor. "The rage for dueling here has reached an incredible and scandalous point," wrote a French observer. Thomas Conway, another general who had been critical of Washington (and who may have been involved in a plot to overthrow him), was challenged to a duel by General John Cadwalader, who shot Conway in the mouth. Conway survived. "I have stopped that damned rascal's lying tongue, at any rate," Cadwalader boasted.

Laurens's duel with Lee took place outside of Philadelphia. They fired at each other from five paces. Lee was hit in the side. The seconds rushed in to end the duel, but the wounded Lee waved them off. He wanted to go another round. Hamilton was scandalized. In his eyes, honor had already been served. By going forward, Lee was indulging in personal enmity toward Laurens. Lee at first insisted, but eventually backed down. Hamilton was pleased with the outcome. The point of a duel, after all, was not to kill someone, but to resolve a dispute in a way that left everyone's honor intact.

It took Burr months to recuperate from the Battle of Monmouth. Eventually he took up a new post in New York's Westchester County. He was serving under Colonel Alexander McDougall, the man who had made Hamilton an artillery captain. Westchester County was a no-man's land between British and colonial lines. Known as the "neutral ground," it was plagued by guerrilla warfare, looting, and intimidation. Vigilantes on both sides sowed terror. It was the Tory "cowboys" against the patriot "skinners." Their raids were more about profit and revenge than about the war.

Burr's role was to try to keep order. He approached it with imagination and discipline. He instituted a register of names that categorized people's allegiance, and the degree of their fervor, so he could track who was doing what. He mapped the countryside, identified hiding places, and recruited young men into an informal intelligence corps. The success of this systematic approach would inform his grassroots approach to politics in the future.

Burr, however, was unhappy with the assignment and eventually resigned his commission in February 1779. He cited his health as the reason, and indeed, he was still quite sick. "I was then so low as to be unable to walk 50 yards," he wrote later, adding that he was "wavering between life and death for the next 18 months." He was also angry over Washington's treatment of Lee, and others who had criticized him. In addition, he clearly felt his own treatment at Washington's hands had been shabby. He believed he should have been promoted faster and higher, and that he would be better off to be out of the army entirely.

Hamilton also had a falling-out with Washington, although it proved to be temporary. Thrown together in close quarters for four years, their relationship had grown testy. One day Washington upbraided Hamilton for making him wait. The hotheaded Hamilton, always touchy about presumed slights, bristled at the general's remark and quit on the spot. Nor was he content to do so quietly. He wrote to a friend that his anger at Washington had been building for a long time. "For three years I have felt no friendship for him and have professed none." Hamilton was piqued at not having been appointed to a field command or some other position of honor. As would happen throughout his career, his anger at the perceived injustice boiled over. Though he was still under twenty-five years old, he had made such an impression that there had been talk about sending him on a mission to France, or putting him in charge of the young nation's sputtering finances. Nothing had come of either suggestion, but he was clearly a young man on the rise, no longer satisfied with being an aide. As he had said years before in St. Croix, he had little interest in groveling as a clerk.

While Hamilton and Washington were both clearly irritated with each other, the bond was never broken. Hamilton was smart enough to know that he still needed Washington's friendship and guidance. Washington didn't want to lose Hamilton's energy and imagination. After four years working together so closely, they had an enormous reservoir of mutual respect to draw on. They continued to correspond, and in July 1781, Washington finally gave Hamilton what he wanted: command of a light-infantry battalion. Hamilton hurried to Yorktown, Virginia, in time for the final battle of the war.

General Washington, with the help of his French allies, had bottled up Lord Charles Cornwallis's British Army. As Washington tightened the noose around Cornwallis, Hamilton, reunited with Lafayette, led his regiment on a dramatic nighttime bayonet attack against a British redoubt that made him a certified hero. Cornwallis surrendered on October 19, 1781. When the British troops marched out of Yorktown, their band expressed the shock that many felt by playing "The World Turned Upside Down." The Battle of Yorktown was the last major conflict of the American Revolution, and proved decisive in bringing about an American victory.

Hamilton and Burr emerged from the war as heroes, but their experiences left them with sharply divergent perspectives. Hamilton had found a close ally in General George Washington. Burr felt alienated from the general, and perhaps a bit disdainful of those who flocked to his banner. Those differing points of view would come to color their political affiliations and personal interactions as they were thrown together in the city that was to become the center of America's postwar rebirth: New York.

EIGHT

BATTLING BARRISTERS

Twenty-one years before

Row upon row of redcoats paraded down Bowery Lane in perfect formation, heads held high as they marched toward Royal Navy ships anchored in New York's East River. It was November 25, 1783. A peace treaty had been signed in September, and on this chilly Tuesday morning, British General Guy Carleton was evacuating the last British soldiers in North America. The departure was not without incident. When a British officer tried to tear down an American flag hoisted over a boardinghouse, the proprietor, Mrs. May, bloodied his nose with a broomstick. Defiant British seamen nailed a British flag to a flagpole at the Battery, the fort guarding the tip of New York City, and greased the pole to prevent the flag from being taken down.

Nevertheless, by early afternoon, the British had boarded their ships. American soldiers under General Henry Knox marched in to secure the city. Many marked the contrast. "The troops just leaving us were as if equipped for show," one eyewitness recalled, "and with their scarlet uniforms and burnished arms, made a brilliant display. The troops that marched in, on the contrary were ill clad and weather-beaten and made a forlorn appearance. But then they were *our* troops."

This was the prelude for a joyous victory parade.

New Yorkers rushed to the streets to see General George Washington and New York governor George Clinton, escorted by eight hundred Continental Army troops from New York and Massachusetts, lead a triumphant procession down Broadway. Onlookers crowding the streets wore black and white ribbons on their chests to demonstrate their patriotic fervor. American seamen tore down the signs of taverns patronized by the British. A sailor named John Van Arsdale put cleats on his shoes so he could climb the greased flagpole and replace the hated Union Jack with the Stars and Stripes.

The war was over, but New York City was a wreck after seven years of British occupation. The population of this once-thriving metropolis had fallen by half to twelve thousand people. More than ten thousand Tory colonists who remained loyal to the British had fled rather than risk reprisals. Fire had devastated entire neighborhoods—more than a thousand buildings had burned, including Trinity Church, which was reduced to a scarred shell. The seemingly endless wharves, previously a mainstay of the New York economy, were falling apart. Food was scarce and prices high. One observer, shocked at the outrageous prices being charged, noted that dinner without wine now cost a dollar!

New York would rise again. In the next two years the city would double in size, as refugees returned home to start over and newcomers poured into the city in search of opportunity. Among them were two newly minted attorneys who set up shop in the city shortly after Washington's victory parade: Alexander Hamilton and Aaron Burr.

★ ★ ★

Back in July 1778, shortly after the Battle of Monmouth, George Washington made his headquarters for a few days at a New Jersey estate called the Hermitage. His host was a remarkable woman whose patriotic fervor was undiminished by the fact that she was married to a British officer then serving in Georgia. Her name was Theodosia Prevost. She impressed many of Washington's officers, but none more than Lieutenant Colonel Aaron Burr. A few months later, when Burr was assigned to escort three loyalists to New York City under a flag of truce, Mrs. Prevost traveled with his party in order to take advantage of the armed escort. Mrs. Prevost and Burr soon began a secret romance. After her husband died in the West Indies, Burr married her in 1782.

At the time of their wedding, Burr was just twenty-five. Theodosia was a decade older with two teenage boys, themselves on the cusp of adulthood. Nonetheless, it was a happy match. Theodosia was far more educated than most women of the day, and renowned for her wit. She and Burr shared a passion for books and ideas, trading thoughts on Voltaire, Rousseau, and other great writers of the day. As for her two sons, Frederick and Bartow Prevost, Burr embraced them as if they were his own.

Alexander Hamilton married Elizabeth Schuyler after a whirlwind courtship in 1780, while still serving on Washington's staff. He met her in Morristown, New Jersey, when the army was camped there for the winter. Eliza, as she was known, was visiting the family of her uncle, Dr. John Cochran, the surgeon general of Washington's army. Hamilton's brother officers had teased him about his frequent infatuations, but this time it was for real. "Hamilton is a gone man," reported his fellow aide, Tench Tilghman. Eliza was the daughter of

General Philip Schuyler, a wealthy landowner in upstate New York. At age twenty-three, she was two years younger than Hamilton. Their wedding took place at Schuyler's elegant Georgian mansion in Albany. She was a self-effacing, brown-haired beauty with "lively dark eyes," according to Tilghman. Petite and athletic, she was captivated by Hamilton. She once said her marriage made her "the happiest of women" and she remained devoted to him through his life and fifty years beyond.

By marrying into the Schuyler family, Hamilton allied himself with a powerful New York political faction. He also grew close to Eliza's older sister Angelica Schuyler Church, a vivacious and intelligent woman who enchanted many well-known men of the era, including Benjamin Franklin, Thomas Jefferson, and Lafayette. Angelica and her sister both seemed to have strong feelings for Hamilton—he was frequently the subject of their letters. Angelica once wrote her sister that she loved Hamilton "very much and, if you were as generous as the old Romans, you would lend him to me for a little while." There has been speculation that Hamilton had an affair with his wife's sister, but there is no solid evidence confirming that. They certainly traded numerous warm letters that sometimes bordered on flirtatious in tone. "I seldom write to a lady without fancying the relation of lover and mistress," Hamilton said in one letter. "It has a very inspiring effect." It is possible to make too much of this. Men and women of the eighteenth century often expressed friendship in terms that strike our twenty-first-century ears as romantic. Not to mention that Angelica was in Europe for the first fifteen years of Hamilton's marriage. If there was some kind of affair, it did not affect the powerful bond between the two sisters, or Hamilton's close business relationship with Angelica's husband, well-to-do businessman John Barker Church.

It was in July of 1781 that Eliza Hamilton probably first met the man who would one day face her husband at Weehawken. Hamilton had just left for Yorktown, and Eliza was pregnant with their son Philip, who was born the following January. Aaron Burr presented himself at the Schuylers' Albany mansion, carrying a letter of introduction to Eliza's father from her husband's and Burr's former commander, Alexander McDougall. "This will be handed to you by Lieutenant Colonel Burr, who goes to Albany, to solicit a license in our courts." Hamilton undoubtedly crossed paths with Burr in Albany when he returned there from the war. Both were studying law, both were young men in a hurry. Burr worked sixteen hours a day under an exacting Albany attorney to prepare for the bar exam. Hamilton decided to go it alone, giving himself a six-month crash course in the law. During that time, he put together a 177-page workbook full of notes so brilliant that other lawyers copied it and used it as a reference in succeeding decades.

In New York at that time, lawyers generally had to serve a three-year apprenticeship before appearing in court. Burr persuaded the New York Supreme Court to waive this training period for returning veterans who had begun their studies before the war. He and Hamilton both took advantage of the ruling to pass the bar and open their own practices after just a few months of study. When the British evacuated New York, they each seized the opportunity to move their practice there.

The New York of 1783 was a tiny place compared to today, about 350 acres of land on the tip of lower Manhattan, barely extending beyond where Houston Street is now. Burr launched his practice from a house at 3 Wall Street, just two doors down from City Hall. Hamilton and his wife, with their infant son, moved into a house down the street, at 57 Wall Street. They were young men on the rise: Hamilton was twenty-eight, Burr just twenty-seven.

An early portrait of Burr depicted an astonishingly guileless, open face with piercing hazel eyes. His gaze "made his presence felt," said one observer. His head seemed almost too big for his slight frame. He tended to favor conservative clothes, and for this portrait he wore a dark coat with a carelessly knotted neck stock. His delicate features made him look even younger than his years, despite a receding hair-line. His hair was just a bit tousled, and overall the look was one of nonchalant elegance.

Hamilton always stood ramrod straight, perhaps to emphasize his military bearing. His flashing blue eyes, offset by his auburn red hair, radiated energy. He believed that "smart dress is essential" and took his look seriously. He favored colorful clothes, and his bills show that some were purchased from a French tailor. A 1792 portrait showed him wearing a golden three-piece suit with matching gloves, fine lace at his throat. A guest at one party described him as wearing a blue coat with bright buttons over a gleaming vest. His hair was always just so. His son James recalled that he had it dressed by a hairdresser every day.

The legal community was a small one—there were only a couple of dozen lawyers practicing in the city. Burr and Hamilton were thrown together by day in courtrooms, by night in the drawing rooms of mutual friends. Sometimes they argued cases against each other, sometimes as co-counsel. Both were successful, but took very differ-ent approaches. Hamilton was combative in court, wearing down the other side with beautifully realized but lengthy arguments. He was already exhibiting the take-no-prisoners style that was to alienate so many. "He was not content with knocking [his opponent] in the head," said his friend and fellow attorney Robert Troup, but "persisted until he had banished every little insect that buzzed around the ears." The urbane Burr tended to be more persuasive, tapping into the emotions of jurors. He was also much briefer in his delivery. "Burr would say as much in half an hour as Hamilton in two hours," said one observer who knew and admired them both. Attorney John Van Ness Yates, watching them both in court one day, said that Hamilton appealed to the head, while Burr "enslaved the heart." Hamilton himself was fascinated and at the same time perplexed by Burr's courtroom performances. He found Burr's style "concise" and "pleasing," but added, "When I analyzed his arguments, I could never discern in what his greatness consisted."

Many of the cases they argued stemmed from the war. The New York legislature passed laws that stacked the deck against remaining Tories. The Confiscation Act called for the seizure of Tory estates. The Trespass Act made it easier to sue Tories for damages inflicted during the war. Other laws had the effect of stripping property rights from those who had been British loyalists. Despite his patriotic fervor, Hamilton took up the cause of Tories who felt their property rights were being threatened. "Legislative folly has afforded so plentiful a harvest to us lawyers that we have scarcely a moment to spare." He was strongly opposed to the new laws, which he thought represented the work of the mob, or "levelers" as he called them, who threatened the social order. He also thought that they conflicted with the Treaty of Paris, and successfully argued that a state should not have the right to supersede a treaty negotiated by the national government. Ever ready with his pen, always happy to make an argument, he dashed off a pamphlet maintaining that attacks on rights and property of people who had sided with the British would hurt the government and the economy, and pave the way for mob rule.

Hamilton's efforts on behalf of the hated Tories began to earn him a reputation as an elitist, sympathetic to the British. One newspaper in New York expressed outrage that Hamilton would assist "the scoundrels of the universe" in this way. Burr also argued a number of these cases, but he tended to take the other side. He thought the laws passed by the legislature were just measures to help people whose property had been devastated in the war to fund their recovery. One of his biggest clients was his wartime commander, William Malcolm, a wealthy New York merchant. Hamilton could not have failed to note that Burr's position was also more the politically popular one at the time.

On a personal level, the two men seemed to get along just fine. They visited one another's homes. Their wives became acquainted. They worked together to help found Erasmus School Academy, a school which lives on today as Erasmus Hall High School. Hamilton, describing Burr to a client in January 1785, called him a man "of influence and abilities." A few months later, both lawyers were arguing cases in the town of Chester, New York, when Burr took a moment to let Hamilton know that he had found out the house Hamilton was renting was up for sale. Delighted, Hamilton promptly wrote Eliza, back in New York City, asking her go ahead and buy it. One mutual acquaintance said later that he never saw the "demon of discord" divide them.

Hamilton was involved in more than just trying cases. He was also the prime mover in the founding of New York City's first bank. He was acting on behalf of his brother-in-law, John Barker Church, who had founded the country's first chartered bank in Philadelphia three years earlier. Hamilton thought such a bank would be a boon to commerce, and threw himself into the project. The bank was started in February 1784. Hamilton and Burr's former commander, Alexander McDougall, now a war hero and a prominent New Yorker, was named bank president. Hamilton became a director, and was also the bank's attorney. Over the next three weeks, Hamilton drafted a constitution for the new institution that became a model for other banks.

In our time, when banks are numerous, and credit easily available, it is hard to understand how controversial banks were in Hamilton's time. Banking was regarded as a sort of black art. Ninety-five percent of the population lived in rural areas, and many of those people looked on banking as something that benefited rich speculators and merchants to the detriment of agricultural interests. Critics suggested that the bank would mainly help the wealthy Tories whose cases Hamilton had argued in court, and shut out farmers. The state legislature denied Hamilton's petition for a charter, so the Bank of New York opened as a private bank in June 1784. It proved enormously successful, so much so that it is still operating today, as BNY Mellon, a monument to Hamilton and his cofounders.

Politics continued to occupy both Hamilton and Burr. Hamilton remained unwavering in his belief that a strong national government was a necessity. While still an officer in the army, and continuing through his law studies, Hamilton authored a series of pamphlets printed under the pseudonym "The Continentalist." Anonymous pamphlets and articles on political questions were common at the time, a way of making powerful and sometimes vitriolic arguments with some degree of deniability—not unlike social media today. In his essays, Hamilton argued that the fledgling nation was doomed unless a "'WANT OF POWER IN CONGRESS' was remedied." The nation was limping along with a weak national government at the mercy of the states. Hamilton wanted to flip the script.

Hamilton's perspective on this issue probably owed something to the fact that he was an immigrant. He had adopted New York as his home, but he did not have the kind of allegiance to a single state that many others did. While some might view Virginia or Pennsylvania as their country of origin, Hamilton knew only one country: the United States. He wanted it to have a government vested with sufficient power to be able to function on its own, and he carried on that argument in the Continental Congress, where he served from 1782 to 1784.

It was here that he teamed up with a like-minded congressman from Virginia who was to become first his trusted associate, and then one of his most formidable opponents. James Madison was shy and bookish. Often dressed in black, he seemed to project no energy, no spark, and he was frequently tongue-tied and gloomy in company. Madison was so frail and diminutive (he was even smaller than Hamilton and Aaron Burr) that he seemed barely capable of carrying on. His physical appearance, however, hid a brilliant intellect and a shrewd mastery of politics. "Never have I seen so much mind in so little matter," said one observer. Like Hamilton, he had served under Washington at the Battle of Trenton. They both shared the idea that the nation required a much stronger federal government with a permanent source of income.

The Continental Congress did not have the power to levy taxes. Under the Articles of Confederation, the agreement among the states that was in essence the country's first constitution, it could only "requisition" contributions from the states, and such requisitions were frequently ignored. As George Washington bitterly noted, "Requisitions are actually little better than a jest," adding that state legislatures were likely to "laugh in your face" when called on to heed treaties and other laws passed by Congress. Hamilton and Madison worked together on a resolution allowing the government to impose taxes. Requiring unanimous approval to pass, it was voted down. Hamilton remained committed to the cause, but after serving a single term in Congress, he stepped down to focus on his law practice.

Just as Hamilton was taking a break from politics, Burr was making his political debut. In 1784, he was elected to the New York Assembly on a ticket headed by the ubiquitous Alexander McDougall. Burr was most likely included on the ticket on the basis of his wartime experience, rather than his political views, which were muted.

Hamilton liked to shout his point of view from the mountaintops, exhausting opponents with his arguments. Burr played his cards close to the vest. Writing to his wife, he took to the third person to describe himself: "He is a grave, silent, strange sort of animal, inasmuch that we know not what to make of him." Both were avid readers, but Hamilton was a more prolific and passionate writer. He committed his every opinion to paper, sometimes to his detriment. Burr's default position was to avoid putting things in writing unless he absolutely had to. Hamilton was fire; Burr was ice.

On one issue, Burr and Hamilton found themselves clearly and publicly on the same side. They were both active in efforts to abolish slavery. This despite the fact that both men, like many well-to-do people of the period, were slave owners. Hamilton, who had seen the horrors of slavery at close hand on Caribbean sugar plantations, was a founding member of the New York Society for the Manumission of Slaves, which advocated gradual emancipation. When the Society petitioned the New York legislature to end slavery, Burr not only supported the resulting bill, he called for immediate emancipation. He also opposed bills that would strip from free blacks the right to vote and serve on juries.

In 1785, New York City suffered an economic downturn. New York wasn't the only state having difficulty prospering in the post-Revolution environment. The whole country faced economic chaos. Each state made its own rules, often to the detriment of the others. New York, for example, imposed import taxes on items coming from New Jersey and Connecticut. Seven states issued their own currency. Virginia and Maryland squabbled about navigation rights on the Potomac. An exasperated James Madison wrote to Thomas Jefferson, then minister to France, complaining about "the present anarchy of our Commerce."[3] The Continental Congress, with little authority, could do nothing but argue about it. The crisis touched on Hamilton's recurring fear that the poor and dispossessed would rise up to the detriment of all. It helped prompt him to run for the New York General Assembly in 1786, where he hoped to continue his campaign for a better, stronger federal government.

The dispute between Virginia and Maryland led to a call for a

---

3. The United States purposefully avoided calling its diplomats "ambassadors" because the word was associated with European monarchy, and instead called them ministers. It wasn't until 1893 that the State Department began styling its envoys as ambassadors.

commission to meet in Annapolis "for the purpose of framing such regulation of trade as may be judged necessary to promote the general interest." There were certainly plenty of issues to deal with, but the response was disappointing. A mere twelve commissioners from five states showed up in September 1786 to the "Commission to Remedy Defects of the federal government." They stayed at Mann's Tavern and held a few desultory meetings before coming to the obvious conclusion that they lacked a quorum and couldn't accomplish much of anything. Nevertheless, their brief get-together had a tremendous impact.

Hamilton managed to get appointed to the commission. So did James Madison. Renewing their partnership from their days in Congress, Hamilton and Madison urged their fellow commissioners to do something truly radical before they left Annapolis and went their separate ways: issue a clarion call for a new convention to amend the Articles of Confederation. For years, in pamphlets, in Congress, and in personal letters, Hamilton had argued his case that the Articles of Confederation were not sufficient to the needs of the country, that a better constructed, more powerful central government was required. Now he drafted a powerful resolution specifically calling on the states to send representatives to convene in Philadelphia the following May "to devise such further provisions as shall appear to them necessary to render the constitution of the federal government adequate to the exigencies of the Union." His report noted that the nation faced problems "of a nature so serious, as, in the view of your Commissioners, to render the situation of the United States delicate and critical." Hamilton and Madison successfully convinced all twelve commissioners to approve the resolution.

Their timing was impeccable. As Congress and the various state legislatures examined the proposal, Massachusetts was in the grip of Shays' Rebellion, an armed uprising of farmers in the western part of the state that threatened to spark a civil war. The rebellion sent a shiver through many who believed that only a stronger national government could keep the country from breaking apart. "I do not conceive we can exist long as a nation," wrote Washington, "without having lodged somewhere a power which will pervade the whole Union in as energetic a manner, as the authority of the different state governments extends over the several States."

There was substantial skepticism about a "Grand Convention" to revise the Articles of Confederation. Many state legislatures were reluctant to initiate a process that might reduce their own authority. Members of the Continental Congress were not wild about the idea of giving another body the right to make an end run around them. In the end, however, Congress voted in favor of the idea, as long as it was "for the sole and express purpose of revising the Articles of Confederation." Twelve states eventually decided to send delegates— only Rhode Island stayed away. Appointed as one of the delegates from New York, Hamilton advocated more than just minor changes. He envisioned a radical restructuring of the government. His efforts would place him firmly on one side of a dispute that would divide the nation into warring political parties.

SEVEN

TAKING SIDES

Seventeen years before

In 1687, mathematician Isaac Newton upended the world of science with his groundbreaking book *Principia Mathematica*. He was inspired, in part, by a spectacular comet that blazed through the sky in 1680. In the years before that cosmic happening, the brilliant scientist had retreated into seclusion, left scientific papers unpublished, even dabbled in the pseudoscience of alchemy. The comet reawakened his true genius, prompting him to build a telescope to study the heavens and lay out his bold thinking. Newton's theory of gravity and his three laws of motion revolutionized science and helped unlock the secrets of the universe. His third law of motion is perhaps the one most familiar to our ears: "For every action, there is an equal and opposite reaction." What is true in physics may also apply to human affairs. Newton's third law illuminates and clarifies the tumultuous and acrimonious politics surrounding the birth of the Constitution.

The first action was the creation of a government under the

Articles of Confederation, ratified in 1781. When this government proved weak and ineffective, it generated a reaction: The Constitutional Convention of 1787. The assembled delegates proposed a radically different and much stronger federal government. That sparked still another reaction: fervent opposition from people who felt that taking power away from the states and concentrating it in the hands of a distant regime would threaten the foundations of democracy. This series of actions and reactions created the nation's first political coalitions. Those who favored the Constitution became known as Federalists. Those who thought it conferred too much power on the national government were first known as Anti-Federalists, or sometimes, just Antis. Eventually, as these loose alliances coalesced into the nation's first political parties, the Antis became known as Democrat-Republicans, or just Republicans. The arguments between the Federalists and the Republicans (which continue to resonate today) not only animated the early days of the new republic, they formed the backdrop of the political maneuverings that would drastically transform the relationship between Alexander Hamilton and Aaron Burr.

Fifty-five delegates from twelve states came to Philadelphia in May of 1787 for the Constitutional Convention. They included the two most famous men in America, Benjamin Franklin and George Washington. Many were lawyers, most had served in Congress, and eight were signers of the Declaration of Independence. Certain distinguished men refused to take part. Patrick Henry, for example, declined to attend, saying he "smelt a rat." James Madison, who had worked hard to bring the convention about, believed that the deliberations of those who did come would "decide forever the fate of republican government."

At thirty-two, Alexander Hamilton was one of the youngest delegates, but already well known. Georgia delegate William Pierce noted that he was "deservedly celebrated for his talents" but also that he could be stiff in his personal interactions and exhibited "a degree of vanity that is highly disagreeable." Pierce thought Hamilton a convincing speaker, rather than a blazing orator, and knew that whenever he rose to speak he would take his time. "There is no skimming over the surface of a subject with him, he must sink to the bottom to see what foundation it rests on."

Though he had labored mightily to bring about the convention, Hamilton played a surprisingly modest role in the proceedings. His influence was hampered by the fact that he was a minority of one in the New York delegation. New York's longtime governor George Clinton was already emerging as an ardent Anti-Federalist. He and his allies in the legislature made sure the other two delegates from New York shared this view. John Lansing, the mayor of Albany, and Robert Yates, a judge on the New York Supreme Court, opposed expanding federal power, and brought with them to Philadelphia a distinct distrust of those, like Hamilton, who favored it.

The convention met at the Pennsylvania State House, the building we now call Independence Hall, where the Declaration of Independence had been signed more than a decade earlier. To encourage unfettered debate and discussion, the delegates decided to conduct their deliberations under a strict veil of secrecy. Guards at the doors kept out spectators and journalists, and no one could make copies of official papers without permission. "Had the deliberations been open while going on," wrote Hamilton, "the clamors of faction would have prevented any satisfactory result." But James Madison sat up near the front every single day, writing a meticulous account of the proceedings; others made notes as well. So posterity has a pretty good idea of what went on.

Two opposing plans set the stage for debate. The Virginia plan, drafted by Madison and other members of the Virginia delegation, proposed a dramatic break with the past: a new and powerful national government that would have three branches: executive, legislative, and judiciary. The New Jersey plan, on the other hand, proposed much more limited changes to the Confederation, keeping the states in the driver's seat. Each state would continue to be, in essence, its own country, and the Confederation itself would have very little power over them.

Hamilton's fellow New York delegates, Lansing and Yates, angrily proclaimed that the Virginia plan went too far. "The states will never sacrifice their essential rights to a national government," argued Lansing heatedly. Hamilton thought it didn't go far enough. Rising to his feet on June 18, 1787, he delivered a marathon six-hour speech, outlining his own alternative. Hamilton praised the British government as the best in the world, and looked to it as a model. He proposed a national government with a president and Senate elected for life, reminiscent of the king and the House of Lords in Britain. He saw this as a check on "popular passions...that spread like wild fire and become irresistible." Under Hamilton's proposal, states would be nearly stripped of their sovereignty, with state governors appointed by the federal government. In his final words he declared, "The people begin to be tired of an excess of democracy. And what is even the Virginia Plan but democracy checked by democracy, or pork still, with a little change of sauce."

Hamilton's speech was his only major contribution to the debate. It was an epic fail, a rare one for the rising political superstar. He had advanced a bold plan that simply did not resonate with any of the delegates. Exhausted by his lengthy harangue, the convention adjourned for the day. When it reconvened, delegates simply moved on to other things. Hamilton's speech would haunt him his entire career. Despite the secrecy, garbled versions of it soon leaked out. They provided plenty of ammunition for his critics, who accused him of favoring monarchy over democracy. It is possible that he put forward his proposal as a tactical move to make the Virginia plan seem more moderate, but it is more likely that it sprang from a desire to insulate the people running the country from the passions of the mob and the changing winds of public opinion.

The convention slogged on over the sticky summer months, the windows of the building shuttered in a vain attempt to keep out the heat and mosquitos. Delegates eventually settled on a modified version of the Virginia plan, with a Senate elected by state legislatures and a House of Representatives elected by the people. Gouverneur (pronounced "governeer") Morris, a Pennsylvania delegate who became a lifelong friend and ally to Hamilton, wrote the famous "We the People..." preamble, and played a significant role in finding language to express the ideas around which the convention had coalesced.

Hamilton had misgivings about the nascent Constitution. "I have great doubts whether a national government on the Virginia plan can be made," one delegate recorded him saying. Morris recalled that Hamilton worried that the Constitution "did not contain sufficient means of strength for its own preservation." Despite his doubts, however, he never considered opposing its adoption. It boiled down to a choice between a plan that *might* not work, or "dismemberment of the union." That was an easy call for Hamilton, who had fought long and hard for a stronger national government. Transcending a hardscrabble youth, tempered in wartime, he had learned to seize upon success as he found it, rather than tilting at windmills and failing. Hamilton was a man of strong beliefs and passionate in his advocacy. As he would show time and time again, however, he was unafraid of compromise, as long as his personal honor was not at stake. Then there could be no backing down.

Hamilton threw his full support behind the final document even though, as Madison notes, "No man's ideas were more remote from the plan than his were known to be." He urged every delegate still present to sign it, whether they had voted in favor of it or not, to give it the best possible chance of being enacted. Congress, with some reluctance, forwarded the document to the states, which would each hold a ratification convention. At least nine of the thirteen states would have to approve it for the new Constitution to go into effect.

Today the Constitution is revered as the bedrock of the United Sates government. The original copy, signed by Washington, Madison, Hamilton, and the other delegates, is considered something akin to a sacred text. It sits on display behind bulletproof glass at the National Archives in Washington, D.C. Its lofty opening phrase, "We the People," rings in our national consciousness. Army officers take an oath to "support and defend" it against "all enemies, foreign and domestic." Members of Congress routinely carry a copy of it in their pocket so they can quote from it. When it was introduced to the public in September 1787, however, it was a radical and, some thought, a dangerous proposal that generated instant controversy and fierce opposition. Patrick Henry scorned the "Tyranny of Philadelphia." Hamilton's fellow New York delegate Robert Lansing called it "a triple-headed monster, as deep and wicked a conspiracy as ever was invented in the darkest ages against the liberties of a free people." Virginia delegate George Mason told the convention he would "sooner chop off his right hand" than support the Constitution the way it was written. The stakes were high: How would the new nation be governed? How much power should the federal government have over taxes and commerce? Would a federal judiciary usurp power from the states?

The debate became highly charged in New York even before the Constitutional Convention was over. Lansing and Yates, Hamilton's fellow New York delegates who were Anti-Federalists, abandoned the proceedings in early July, disgusted and disturbed by the direction the deliberations were taking. No longer considering themselves bound by secrecy, they briefed New York governor George Clinton. Word apparently got back to Hamilton that Clinton was already bad-mouthing the plan coming together in Philadelphia. Hamilton was offended by the breach of secrecy, not to mention what he saw as Clinton's attempt to poison the well before the Constitution was even finalized. In typical Hamilton style, he launched a preemptive attack, all guns blazing. His choice of weapon was a barbed anonymous essay (which he later admitted writing) that called Clinton "thick-skulled and double-hearted" and charged the governor with being more interested in his own power than in the public good.

Action, reaction. The gloves were off. Clinton allies responded in kind, with essays labeling Hamilton "Tom Shit" (the newspapers used asterisks to avoid printing the vulgar word). They accused him of being a lowborn "upstart attorney" with African ancestry. They struck at Hamilton's pride by insinuating that during the war he had managed to "palm himself" off on George Washington, who had unceremoniously fired him once he found out that Hamilton was "a superficial, self-conceited coxcomb." Hamilton, deeply wounded, called on Washington to deny the charges, which he did. The sniping illustrates how Hamilton's brash, combative style polarized debate and hardened his enemies against him. Continuing for months, it opened a yawning political divide between Hamilton and Clinton that was to have serious repercussions.

As opposition mounted to the Constitution, Hamilton threw himself into defending it. In September 1787, he launched the first in a series of newspaper articles making the case for ratification, a series that became famous as *The Federalist Papers*. He recruited fellow Virginia delegate James Madison, and New York's John Jay, then serving as secretary of foreign affairs, to write the essays. They painted a vivid picture of the disasters that would befall the country by continuing under the Articles of Confederation, and contrasted them in sharp detail with the benefits of the new Constitution. To avoid flouting the secrecy rules of the convention, they wrote under the pseudonym *Publius*. The name could not have been more apt. Five hundred years before the time of Julius Caesar, Publius Valerius led a Roman revolution, overthrowing the monarchy to set up a republican form of government.

Hamilton originally planned for twenty-five articles, but the project soon ballooned. Over the next six months, the three men would write and publish eighty-five essays. Jay penned five before dropping out for health reasons. Madison wrote twenty-nine. Hamilton authored an astounding fifty-one. It was a herculean effort. After fortifying himself with strong coffee, Hamilton would sit for six hours or more hunched over his desk, quill pen in hand, writing ceaselessly. It was advocacy journalism, and the deadlines were brutal. The printer would sometimes stand in his office waiting for him to finish so that the handwritten drafts could be set into type.

The Federalist Papers are rightfully celebrated as one of Hamilton's signature achievements. Taking nothing away from Madison and Jay's contributions, the series as a whole is a testament to Hamilton's stamina and brilliance. His contributions show a man determined to leave no stone unturned in his crusade on behalf of the Constitution. The influence of *The Federalist Papers* was felt in both the New York and Virginia ratifying conventions. *The Federalist Papers* would play an even more important role in the decades and centuries that followed ratification, offering scholars, lawyers, and judges a unique glimpse into the thinking that animated the content of the Constitution.

In April 1788, New York held elections to choose delegates to the state ratifying convention. Hamilton was among nineteen Federalist delegates elected primarily from the New York City area. Governor Clinton and the Anti-Federalists elected forty-six delegates, an overwhelming majority. In addition, Governor Clinton himself would chair the convention. The deck seemed stacked against New York Federalists, but that only energized Hamilton, who vowed to his supporters that he would not give up, whatever the odds. "Tell them the convention shall never rise until the Constitution is adopted."

By the time the New York convention convened in June at a two-story stone courthouse in Poughkeepsie, eight other states had already ratified the Constitution. Under the rules set out by Congress, the Constitution would take effect once it was ratified by one more state. New York and Virginia, the two largest states, and therefore the two most important, were giving simultaneous consideration to the question. James Madison, a delegate to the Virginia convention, agreed to stay in close touch with Hamilton.

Four days into the convention, news arrived that New Hampshire had become the ninth state to ratify. The "more perfect union" would now be established with those nine states, and any others that ratified. That changed the terms of debate. The question was no longer over the details of the arrangements, but whether or not New York would join the Union.

Hamilton was a whirlwind of activity. He spoke twenty-six times, more than any other Federalist. He dissected passages and explained meanings, doing so not only with the aim of erasing doubts about the document under consideration, but also to buy time in the hope that there would soon be good news from Virginia that would help sway opinion. Tempers ran high. John Lansing accused Hamilton of secretly advocating the abolishment of states. Hamilton's response was so angry that debate was halted for the day to let everyone calm down. On another occasion, after a making heated speech, Hamilton made a rare apology for being too "vehement" in his arguments, saying his "strong expressions" were prompted by the "interesting nature of the subject."

On July 2, a horseman galloped up to the courthouse in Poughkeepsie. He had ridden nine hours from New York City, the last leg in a journey from Virginia, with a letter for Hamilton from James Madison. In a dramatic scene worthy of Hollywood or the Broadway stage, Hamilton stood and read it out loud to the hushed delegates. Virginia had ratified the Constitution! The Federalists rose from their seats and left the hall for an impromptu celebration outside the building.

The news increased the pressure on the Anti-Federalists. Still, debate on whether to ratify dragged on. The anger on display in

Poughkeepsie began to spread. Two days later, on July 4, a bloody riot broke out in Albany. A copy of the Constitution was put to the torch. Federalists and Anti-Federalists cracked heads, killing one man and wounding eighteen more. Hamilton, pointing to the relentless tumult, proclaimed to the convention that New York City might secede if the state did not vote for the Constitution. Clinton chastised him for this "highly indiscreet and improper warning." Finally, by the narrowest of votes, the delegates ratified the Constitution—with the caveat that they expected Congress to take up a Bill of Rights as soon as possible, to guard against the federal government having too much power. Though it took two more years, the last two holdout states, North Carolina and Rhode Island, eventually joined the new nation as well. Hamilton had won the battle for ratification. He had played a pivotal role in bringing about a radical change in government. In the process, however, he had created numerous political enemies and made himself a lightning rod for controversy.

Where was Aaron Burr in all this? Practicing law in New York City. Hamilton had more to say about the Constitution during this period than anyone in the country; his sheer output of words both written and spoken is exhausting to contemplate. Burr was virtually silent. "When the Constitution was in deliberation, his conduct was equivocal," wrote Hamilton five years later. There are clues to suggest Burr was an Anti-Federalist, but he kept his head down. He turned down a chance to run as a delegate to the ratification convention, probably because he knew he would lose—no Anti-Federalist was elected from New York City. Ever the pragmatist, though, he understood that once Virginia ratified the Constitution, it was "politic and necessary" that New York should do the same. "I think it a fortunate event and the only one that could preserve the peace," he wrote to a friend. Then, almost as an afterthought, he added: "It is highly probable that New York will be for some time the seat of the federal government."

On the afternoon of April 30, 1789, New York Chancellor Robert Livingston administered the presidential oath to George Washington at New York's Federal Hall. The nation's first president elected under the Constitution (there had been eight presidents under the Articles of Confederation) swore the oath on a Bible that had been hastily procured at a local Masonic lodge that morning when event organizers realized they didn't have one. After reciting the oath of office prescribed in the Constitution, Washington impulsively added the words "So help me God," setting a precedent for every president to follow. Federalists and Anti-Federalists put aside their arguments to take part in the celebrations. Aaron Burr called that first inauguration "a day of glee."

There was so much to do. Everything had to be created from scratch. No one even knew what to call George Washington. Many people, Vice President John Adams foremost among them, thought that referring to Washington as "president" simply was not suitably august. "Fire brigades and cricket clubs have presidents," Adams exclaimed in disgust. He argued that it was important to give the highest office in the land a title with more "dignity and splendor." South Carolina senator Ralph Izard proposed calling the president "His Excellency." George Washington initially favored the title "His High Mightiness." The Senate spent weeks debating this issue, before the House made it clear that "president" would suffice. There were countless other details to hammer out as well.

Washington was organizing the executive branch. One of the key posts he had to fill was secretary of the treasury. Financial problems had crippled his army and then brought about the demise of the Confederation. Treasury, then, was perhaps the most critical post in the new government. Washington offered it to Robert Morris Jr., a Philadelphia merchant who had helped finance the Revolution. Morris declined, running for the Senate instead. He recommended a "far cleverer fellow" for the post: Alexander Hamilton. Washington seemed taken aback. "I always knew Colonel Hamilton to be a man of superior talents, but never supposed that he had any knowledge of finance."

"He knows everything, sir," Morris supposedly replied.

There was never any doubt that Washington would want Hamilton as a top adviser. Though nine years had passed since Yorktown, they remained in frequent touch and were close allies. Hamilton had been instrumental in convincing the reluctant Washington that he must run for president. The only question was where he would serve. The decision by Morris to turn down Treasury made that an easy one. Soon after the inaugural, Washington told Hamilton that he was going to name him treasury secretary. Hamilton's appointment would have to wait until the House and Senate approved legislation establishing the Treasury Department. That left him plenty of time to get himself in trouble dabbling in New York politics.

Barely half a dozen years after the end of the Revolution, the New York political scene was a confusing tangle of shifting alliances. There were three powerful families: the Schuylers, the Livingstons, and the Clintons. Early Burr biographer James Parton summed up the scene this way: "The Clintons had *power*, the Livingstons had *numbers*, and the Schuylers had *Hamilton*." A colorful description that contained more than a grain of truth. Hamilton had married into the Schuyler family and become its most influential political leader. But the landscape was changing.

Flush with his victory in the ratifying convention, Hamilton set his sights on Governor George Clinton, who controlled New York politics in his viselike grip. Hamilton feared that Clinton would try to undermine the new federal government, and he could not forget the smear campaign against him from the previous year. In February 1789, Hamilton organized a public meeting to rally support around an opposition candidate. Hamilton's choice was a shocker: Judge Robert Yates, who had fought Hamilton and the Constitution at the conventions in Philadelphia and Poughkeepsie. Since ratification he had come around and Hamilton considered him a moderate candidate, "better calculated to heal divisions."

One of the people joining Hamilton in support of Yates was Aaron Burr. For the moment, Burr and Hamilton were on the same team. It turned out to be the losing team, as the popular Clinton beat back the challenge and won reelection to another three-year term. The net result of the campaign was simply to intensify the enmity between Hamilton and Clinton.

The alliance between Hamilton and Burr strengthened over the summer, though, as Burr wrote to Hamilton from Albany, keeping him abreast of activities in the legislature. Then, in the fall, Governor Clinton drove a wedge into that relationship by appointing Burr as attorney general of New York.

Clinton had just survived a major challenge and was trying to bring an able young player from the opposing side over to his team. Burr, as he would do throughout his career, was acting as an independent, unwilling to be strongly allied with any one faction, feeling free to move between them. He had joined with the Federalists to support

Yates, a close personal friend, but he had no qualms about switching sides to work for Clinton. Did this expose him as a man who lacked fixed principles? Or did it demonstrate savvy political pragmatism? Political alliances had yet to harden into party politics, but it is easy to envision Alexander Hamilton shaking his head at what must have seemed like perfidy from a man with whom he had a personal and professional relationship.

Hamilton also inserted himself in the New York Senate race. Although they had not defeated Clinton, the Federalists did manage to win control of the legislature. Since the legislature picked United States senators in those days, it was clear that both senators from New York would be Federalists. The Schuylers and the Livingstons, both in the Federalist camp, cooked up a plan to divide the seats between them. One would go to Philip Schuyler, Hamilton's father-in-law. He in turn would lend his support to a candidate backed by the Livingston family. Seemingly a win-win plan, until Hamilton threw a wrench in the works. He convinced his father-in-law to renege on his pledge and instead back Massachusetts transplant Rufus King, who had served as a delegate from that state to the Constitutional Convention. Hamilton likely thought King, who had been a strong voice at the convention, would be a valuable ally in the Senate.

This time Hamilton stepped in it. Action, reaction. King was elected senator, but Robert Livingston was infuriated. A powerful voice in favor of ratification, he now felt betrayed by Hamilton. He was made even more furious when Hamilton, jealously guarding his own political power base, thwarted Livingston's effort to get a major appointment in the new federal government. Livingston broke with Hamilton and the Schuylers, and aligned himself with Governor Clinton. They both wanted to chasten the new treasury secretary, and they knew just how to do it. The first people elected to the Senate all had staggered terms. By luck of the draw, some had two years, some four, some six. Philip Schuyler got two, so his term would be up in 1791. Clinton and Livingston plotted a takedown of Hamilton's father-in-law, whom they considered to be Hamilton's "supple jack"—that is, someone who would bend to Hamilton's will. Clinton handpicked a candidate to challenge Schuyler, a talented and personable lawyer not strictly identified with any faction.

The candidate: Aaron Burr.

When Schuyler's term was up in 1791, Clinton engineered his defeat and Burr's election with a series of backroom deals that one observer described as "full of twistings, combinations and maneuvers." Not long before, Hamilton and Burr had supported the same candidate, and Burr had been sending Hamilton letters with the latest political news. Now, Burr not only seemed to have found a home with the opposition camp, he had helped humiliate Hamilton's father-in-law and replace him as senator from New York. It was a blow both political and personal. And Hamilton had set it in motion through his own blunders and miscalculations.

Burr had done the unpardonable. Hamilton would not forget.

SIX

POWER STRUGGLES

Fourteen years before

Thomas Jefferson was about to stroll into the four-story brick mansion on Broadway that served as President Washington's official residence, when he bumped into Alexander Hamilton. The year was 1790, and spring was just about to turn into summer. The two men had only met for the first time three months before. Jefferson, freshly returned from France, was the new secretary of state in Washington's cabinet. He was taken aback by Hamilton's appearance. Jefferson thought the secretary of the treasury looked "somber, haggard, and dejected beyond description." His clothes were a mess. In short, he was a wreck. Hamilton asked if he could speak to Jefferson, and the two men conducted an extraordinary tête-à-tête on the bustling New York thoroughfare.

Hamilton was fighting to enact legislation that he deemed critical to the survival of the new nation. He was wrapped in gloom and despair because he was staring defeat in the face, a defeat he thought might be a mortal wound to the new government. Gone was Hamilton's self-confidence, bordering on cockiness, that was his trademark. He told Jefferson he was at his wit's end, that if the bill failed he might quit his post. He begged for help. Jefferson's response? He invited Hamilton to dinner—a dinner that was to prove to be a pivotal moment in American history.

Hamilton took over as secretary of the treasury in September 1789. He started with just an empty office suite. There were a vast number of things to do, and every decision set a precedent. From the beginning, his most important job was to put the new nation on a firm financial footing. This was a subject he had been studying and brainstorming about since his time as Washington's aide during the Revolutionary War. He threw himself into it. Three months after starting the job, he presented Congress with an audacious and well-thought-out financial plan contained in his fifty-one-page "Report on Public Credit."

That's when all hell broke loose.

The linchpin of Hamilton's plan involved public debt. There was a pile of it, a tangled mess dating back to the Revolution. The national government was mired in debt because Congress had been powerless to levy taxes to pay its bills. Many of the states had also incurred huge debts fighting the war. A sizable amount consisted of IOUs to soldiers and contractors from that war. Some of the debt was domestic, some of it foreign, involving various currencies and interest rates. The weight of it threatened to drag down the new nation.

Hamilton's complex plan boiled down to three simple ideas: (1) The federal government should assume the debts of the states. (2) It should issue new government bonds to pay all debts in full. (3) It should dedicate specific tax revenues to pay off those bonds. Put another way, the new government would borrow huge amounts of money (in the form of bonds) to pay not only its own debts, but also to assume the debts of the states. Since the national government already had $50 million of debt to wrestle with, it may seem odd that Hamilton proposed to burden it with an additional $25 million in debt from the states. Hamilton had the genius to discern that the debt was not a problem. It was an opportunity.

Benjamin Franklin once opined that the best way to make a friend is to ask a favor. It sounds counterintuitive. Shouldn't you *do* someone a favor if you want to be their friend? But that's not how Franklin saw it. "He that has once done you a kindness will be more ready to do you another, than he whom you yourself have obliged."

Franklin's shrewd observation was that once someone did you a favor, they considered themselves an ally, invested in your success. Hamilton approached the debt crisis from a similar perspective. By borrowing money through the sale of bonds, the government would be making friends.

Abroad, the plan would reestablish America's shaky credit standing, encouraging foreign investment. Hamilton was persuaded that this was essential in order for the new country to thrive. At home, it would help convince people to support federal taxes, still a controversial idea that aroused angry opposition. Investors both foreign and domestic would have a powerful financial incentive to make sure the new government succeeded—and less incentive to back the states against the government in any sort of political showdown. Trading in government bonds would also create a credit market that might stimulate private credit and help jump-start the economy.

No surprise: Hamilton's plan engendered vehement opposition.

Some of the states, such as Virginia, had already paid off their debt and thought Hamilton's plan was unfair. Other detrators saw the plan as a corrupt giveaway. Many soldiers and businesses owed money by the states had traded away their IOUs for pennies on the dollar. Paying those debts in full would be a windfall bailout for the speculators who had bought them up. Many of the speculators, critics suspected, were Hamilton's political allies, cynically supporting a bill that would help enrich them. One Republican congressman referred contemptuously to the "Report on Public Credit" as Hamilton's "gambling report," and feared it would lead to rampant speculation that could undermine the fragile new economy. The vast majority of Americans living in rural areas tended to believe that real wealth was created by hardworking farmers. It seemed to them that Hamilton's plan tilted away from farmers and toward moneyed elites in the big cities.

Hamilton's plan awoke an even deeper dread among those who feared a concentration of power in the federal government, especially the executive branch. Some saw it as a cynical power grab that would lead to a dangerous marriage between moneyed interests and the government..It would encourage more federal spending and cement the dominance of the federal government over the states. Opposition was especially strong in the rural South. Some there compared the assumption of state debt to the hated Stamp Act imposed by the British before the Revolution, and hinted at secession. The soon-to-be governor of Virginia, Henry Lee, urged bold and precipitous action, writing, "It seems to me that we southern people must be slaves in effect, or cut the Gordian knot at once."

In some ways it was the argument about the Constitution all over again, but the players were shifting. Some who favored ratification, like Henry Lee, thought Hamilton had gone too far. Hamilton was shocked to see his former collaborator, James Madison, emerging as a fierce opponent of his plan. Hamilton thought he and Madison were in perfect agreement, and later said he never would have taken the Treasury job if he dreamed Madison would oppose him.

Elected as a congressman from Virginia, Madison had become a powerful leader in the House of Representatives. He had drafted and pushed through a Bill of Rights, and had earned the nickname the "Big Knife" for his ability to cut deals. His opposition was a major obstacle. Representing Virginia's well-being, Madison was concerned that Hamilton's plan would be unfair to his state. Beyond that, it awakened fears in Madison that speculators would hijack the new government. "I go on the principle that a public debt is a public curse," wrote Madison. And he thought it would siphon power and influence from Congress and route it toward the executive branch—and, not incidentally, Alexander Hamilton himself.

The fight over debt assumption turned into what Jefferson called "the most bitter and angry contest ever known in Congress before or since the union of the states." It seemed as if the very idea of union was threatened. Passions ran high.

In the midst of this fight, a hotheaded South Carolina congressman named Aedanus Burke publicly branded Hamilton a liar, ostensibly because Hamilton had belittled southern militiamen at the funeral of General Nathanael Greene. An angry exchange of letters followed, escalating tensions. "The town is much agitated about a duel between Burke and Hamilton," wrote Pennsylvania senator William Maclay in his diary. "So many people concerned in the business may really make the fools fight." Sensitive to his illegitimate birth, fiercely proud of the reputation he had built up, Hamilton remained prickly about anything that touched upon his honor. Eventually, a group of congressmen negotiated a satisfactory end to the dispute without the two men having to shoot it out. As Hamilton undoubtedly knew, this is how most "affairs of honor" were resolved—only a fraction of such quarrels ended in actual bloodshed.

Although seemingly unrelated to the financial debate, the Burke affair showed how divided and angry the warring factions were. After much wrangling, and several votes in the House, Hamilton found himself on the losing side. By June of 1790 his plan was in danger of being cast aside. That's when he ran into Jefferson outside of Washington's mansion.

At six feet two Thomas Jefferson towered over both Hamilton and Madison. A decade older than either, he was also a respected statesman who had served as the governor of Virginia and minister to France. We remember him today as the primary author of the Declaration of Independence, but that was not yet widely known. Jefferson cut a memorable figure, tall and slender, a "straight-up" man, according to one of his slaves, with hazel eyes and red hair. (As president, he once received a letter that opened with the salutation "You red-headed son of a bitch.") He was an enigmatic figure. John Adams recalled that during the debates over the Declaration of Independence, he never heard Jefferson say more than three sentences together. At times he seemed to want nothing more than to retreat to Monticello with his books. Yet he was a brilliant political philosopher and writer, a passionate champion of individual liberty over the tyranny of a distant central government, and a shrewd political player.

Jefferson was a latecomer to this battle. He had been in office only a few months, after spending years in France. There he had observed with satisfaction the initial rumblings of the French Revolution, and flirted with Hamilton's vivacious sister-in-law, Angelica Schuyler Church. (In fact, Jefferson's copy of *The Federalist Papers* was one that Hamilton's wife had given to her sister, who had in turn passed it along.) Jefferson was a reluctant supporter of the Constitution, wary about concentrating so much power in the hands of the federal government. Assumption definitely set off warning bells in his head, but his time in Europe had given him a practical understanding of the repercussions that might ensue if Hamilton's plan was voted down. "Our credit [in Europe] will burst and vanish," he wrote. He further predicted that such a dire situation could lead to chaos: the states might splinter, each devising its own payment terms, some defaulting on debt entirely, prompting Europeans to stay away from any financial dealings across the Atlantic.

Jefferson invited Madison and Hamilton to a private dinner at his lodgings on Maiden Lane. It was to be a private affair—just the three of them. Jefferson told them that his "object was to find some temperament for the present fever," adding that "sound heads and honest views needed nothing more than explanation and mutual understanding to enable them to unite." He went on to say that having only recently returned from France, he didn't understand the debt issue particularly well, and encouraged them to consider the thing together.

Jefferson's account of the evening is the only one we have, and it is short on details. One can imagine that there was a certain degree of tension masked by surface cordiality. Jefferson was well aware that passage of Hamilton's bill would be a bitter pill for opponents. Luckily, he had a good idea of what might help make the medicine go down.

At the same time that the assumption battle was raging, Congress was arguing another question: where to locate the new national capital. Sixteen different sites had been proposed. The metropolitan northern cities New York and Philadelphia were the frontrunners. Southerners feared that locating the capital in a big northern city would give undue influence to bankers and merchants. They favored a location along the Potomac River between Virginia and Maryland. Many of these same southerners opposed Hamilton's plan. The fact that Hamilton's opponents sometimes referred to New York as "Hamiltonopolis" demonstrates how closely they identified the secretary of the treasury and his financial plan with the commercial interests of New York City.

Jefferson later wrote that he could not recall who suggested the quid pro quo. By the time they had finished the meal and tossed off the last glass of wine, however, a deal was in place. Madison would allow Hamilton's financial plan to pass; Hamilton would throw his support to the southern location for the capital. Such a deal had already been whispered about in secret meetings and furtive conversations, but the dinner put the finishing touches on it. The Compromise of 1790, as it became known, paved the way for Hamilton's plan to take effect, and for Washington, D.C., to become the permanent capital. Philadelphia would serve as a temporary capital for ten years.

It is viewed today as one of the great political triumphs of American history, cooler heads prevailing to execute a compromise that saved the union. There was, however, violent reaction to it in some quarters. Typical was the Virginia resolution proclaiming that Hamilton's plan would prostrate "agriculture at the feet of commerce" or possibly be "fatal to the existence of American Liberty."

By the time he wrote about the dinner two years later, Jefferson had come to regret what he had done. He claimed he had been "duped" by Hamilton, and that he had only gone along with the plan "from a fear of disunion, while our government was still in its most infant state." By that time Congress had also approved Hamilton's proposal for a National Bank. "It enabled Hamilton so to strengthen himself by corrupt services to many, that he could afterwards carry his bank scheme," said Jefferson. He thought Hamilton had turned the United States into a "gaming table" with madcap speculating by a "corrupt squadron of paper dealers." The divisions separating the Federalists and the Republicans were growing ever more clear: Urban versus rural. Commercial versus agrarian. New York versus Virginia.

Hamilton versus Jefferson.

Jefferson was to become Hamilton's towering political nemesis, a rival of a far different order than Burr. While Hamilton and Burr competed in politics and the courtroom, Jefferson was an intellectual colossus who would bestride the scene as Hamilton's towering ideological adversary. The two men spent four years together in Washington's cabinet. They began as cordial friends—Hamilton held a welcoming dinner for Jefferson at his house—but by the time Jefferson left the cabinet they were barely speaking to each other. Their views on the proper role of government diverged so widely that the words "Jeffersonian" and "Hamiltonian" came to represent opposite poles of American politics.

In modern parlance, Hamilton and the Federalists thought government was the solution; Jefferson and the Republicans thought government was the problem. Hamilton wanted a strong federal government to bind the states together, to encourage manufacturing and economic development. Jefferson believed that too much government was a threat to liberty. "Energetic government," he wrote, "is always oppressive." Hamilton's plan, he thought, had "change[d] the political complexion of the government of the U.S." Furthermore, Hamilton's financial system was modeled after the British government. He made no secret of admiring the way that the British administered their finances. Jefferson hated the British, whom he called "rich, proud, hectoring, swearing, squabbling, carnivorous animals," and he commented that Hamilton was "so bewitched and perverted by the British example as to be under thorough conviction that corruption was essential to the government of a nation." He detected in Hamilton's actions a plot to take power away from the states, away from Congress, and put it in the hands of the president, who would be under the influence of mercenaries and speculators "who adhered to Hamilton of course as their leader in that principle."

The two men dreamed different dreams for America, and each saw different monsters lurking under the bed. Jefferson hated monarchy above all things. That can be seen in the harsh words about King George III he wrote in the Declaration of Independence. Monarchy represented the ultimate concentration of power. His time in France, coinciding with the beginnings of the French Revolution against King Louis XVI, only hardened his view. "I was much an enemy to monarchy before I came to Europe," he told George Washington. "I am ten thousand times more so since I have seen what they are." Hamilton, he came to believe, was a dangerous monarchist, and his supporters, who were "itching for crowns, coronets, and miters," had "a preference of kingly over republican government."

Hamilton feared anarchy and mob rule above all things. His vision of America, going back to the Revolution, demanded a strong government led by a powerful executive, not one paralyzed by the spats and rows of Congress. He considered Jefferson to be "a man of profound ambition & violent passions," with views "subversive of the principles of good government and dangerous to the union, peace and happiness of the Country." He worried that if Jefferson and the Republicans prevailed, it would subvert the national government and threaten the stability of the new country.

From entrenched positions, peering at each other over bristling philosophical fortifications, they were engaged in a battle for the soul of America. Who was right? We live in a world that is much closer to Hamilton's vision than Jefferson's. If Hamilton were alive today, he would point to America's incredible economic engine, the financial markets that make credit available to entrepreneurs trying to start new companies, the still-powerful manufacturing sector, and the decades of prosperity created by business and government working together, and say with satisfaction, "Obviously, I was right." If Jefferson were alive today, he would point to the cozy relationship between Wall Street and big government, the power of the 1 percent, the recurring scandals involving financial manipulations and crony capitalism, the protests of citizens who feel that are left behind, and say in agitation, "Obviously, I was right." The argument may never end.

One last ironic footnote to the dinner: the location of Jefferson's home is now the site of the New York branch of the Federal Reserve Bank, the existence of which would outrage the man who once lived there.

As huge as they were, the battles over assumption and the National Bank were only a portion of what occupied Alexander Hamilton at the Treasury. Spending countless hours behind the elegant mahogany desk that he installed in his office, Hamilton had to assemble a new department from scratch. Soon the Treasury had more than forty employees. His opponents charged him with empire building. In fact, his days were filled with endless minutiae. The day following

his momentous dinner with Jefferson and Madison, he wrote to
President Washington, asking him to approve a contract for "timber,
boards, Nails and Workmanship" to replace a beacon near the light-
house in Sandy Hook, New Jersey. He oversaw the creation of the
National Mint, the Customs Service, and the Coast Guard. Perhaps
most important of all, he remained a trusted adviser to the president.
Republicans began to grouse about his sway over President Washington, whose actions showed him in full support of Hamilton's activist
agenda.

With battle lines drawn, and an election year coming up, Jefferson
and Madison set out on a monthlong journey through five northern
states in the summer of 1791. Ostensibly it was a "botanizing tour"
to satisfy their scientific curiosity about unusual plants and flowers in
northern forests. Politics, however, was also on the itinerary during
the thousand-mile expedition. Jefferson and Madison spent at least
some of their time party building, enlisting allies in their fight against
Hamilton and the Federalists. That led them to the new senator from
New York, none other than Aaron Burr.

Burr's 1791 election to the Senate was a blow to Hamilton and
his associates, who clearly regarded him as an obdurate foe. "He is
avowedly your enemy," wrote one concerned New Yorker, telling
Hamilton that Burr "stands pledged to his party, for a reign of vindic-
tive declamation against your measures." In truth, Burr did not seem
particularly fervent in his opposition to Hamilton's plan. He told a
friend that he couldn't even be bothered to read all the arguments for
and against. Nevertheless, he was certainly open to overtures from
Jefferson.

Hamilton went on high alert when one of his friends wrote to say that when Burr met with Madison and Jefferson, the result was a "passionate courtship." Hamilton was convinced "that Mr. Madison, cooperating with Mr. Jefferson, is at the head of a faction decidedly hostile to me and my administration." If Burr was *with* those two, didn't that mean he must be *against* Hamilton? Party lines were hardening, yet in fact Burr resisted committing himself fully to one camp or another. By the time he took up his duties as a senator, the government had moved to Philadelphia. There, he tended to vote Republican, but did not publicly declare himself as such. He was a loner, a political freelancer, appealing to both sides, but fully trusted by none, a pattern that would continue for his entire career.

In the Senate, Burr kept his head down and focused on his committee work. He was particularly interested in foreign affairs, and got permission from Jefferson to let himself into the State Department early each morning to peruse documents there—until George Washington got wind of it and ordered Jefferson to keep him out. Once again, Burr found reason to be resentful of and angry with Washington.

The year 1792 would prove to be a watershed in the relationship between Hamilton and Burr. It began with the New York governor's race. Burr presented himself as an independent candidate, "aloof of party dispersions," trying to attract votes from both Republicans and Federalists. In a time when party politics was being embraced by some and feared by others, his independent stance won him support in some surprising quarters. "The cautious distance observed by this gentleman toward all parties," wrote one New York Federalist, "may be a real merit in a Governor." Already Burr was talked about as being "industrious in his canvass," paying careful attention to the details of politicking. Hamilton was alarmed by Burr's success in reaching out to Federalists and threw himself in Burr's path. He urged John Jay, by then chief justice of the Supreme Court, to become a candidate.[4] When Jay did so, Burr saw the handwriting on the wall and dropped out of the race.

Yet Burr's involvement in the governor's race was not over. The election came down to three closely contested counties where there were voting irregularities. The New York Board of Canvassers asked the state's two senators, both lawyers of high repute, to render an opinion on how to handle the contested votes. Burr and Federalist Rufus King conferred, but found that they were split along party lines. Burr, wishing to avoid alienating supporters on both sides, attempted to convince King that they should simply keep quiet and decline to give any advice. King didn't agree. He leaped into the fray with an opinion that all the votes cast in those counties should be considered valid, which would throw the election to Jay. Burr was forced to go on record with an opposing view, arguing that most of the votes in those counties should be thrown out. The Board of Canvassers followed Burr's suggestion, which gave the race to Governor George Clinton by just 108 votes.

Republicans thought Burr had issued a sensible and judicious opinion. Federalists accused him of throwing the race to Clinton, a charge he vehemently denied. "Some pretend, indeed, but none can believe,

---

4. The notion of a Supreme Court justice running for political office may strike modern readers as bizarre. It was much more common in colonial times for judges to run for political office. Today, most federal judges are forbidden to take part in political activities. But interestingly enough, those rules do not apply to Supreme Court judges, who are technically still able to endorse a candidate or run for office—though it would likely result in a firestorm of controversy if one actually did so.

that I am prejudiced in his [Clinton's] favor." Stung by the allegations, Burr took what for him was an unusual step. He published a fifty-page defense of his actions and sought help to clear his name. Yet even under attack, he seemed relatively dispassionate, more disappointed than furious at the accusations made against him. "I do not see how any unbiased man can doubt [my innocence]," he wrote to a friend, "but still I do not pretend to control the opinions of others, much less take offense at any man for differing with me." The dispute pushed him further into the Republican camp, and helped boost his national profile just as a presidential election was getting under way.

Once George Washington agreed to run again, it was a foregone conclusion that he would be reelected. The mechanics of presidential elections were very different then, however, and offered the opportunity for some political jockeying with respect to the vice presidency. There was no popular vote. Each state selected two presidential electors. In most states, they were elected by the state legislatures. Each elector cast two ballots. At least one of the ballots had to be for a candidate from another state. Whoever won the most electoral votes became president. The second biggest vote getter became vice president. Jefferson and the Republicans sought to flex their muscles by seeing if they could rally the support of enough electors to unseat Vice President John Adams. Like Hamilton, Adams was a passionate (and prickly) Federalist who thought a strong executive was the "essence of government."

New York governor George Clinton was the Republican considered to have the best chance to defeat Adams, but Burr's name was also floated as an alternative. The ranks of his supporters were growing. "Burrites," they were sometimes called. "Burr's Myrmidons," Hamilton derisively labeled them, using a word that intimated they were unscrupulous ruffians. Burr's admirers urged him on. "Your friends everywhere look for you to take an active part in removing the monarchical rubbish of our government," wrote Benjamin Rush, a physician and leading social reformer from Philadelphia. "It is time to speak out—or we are undone."

Hamilton's response to Burr's candidacy was extreme. He had no love for Governor George Clinton, considering him an enemy of the national government, and thought it would be "very unfortunate" if he won. But he reserved a breathtaking venom for Burr. His rage exploded onto the page in an extended rant he shared privately with his closest allies. Burr was "unprincipled both as a public and private man," Hamilton wrote. "He is for or against nothing, but as it suits his interest or ambition. He is determined, as I conceive, to make his way to be the head of the popular party and to climb . . . to the highest honors of the state; and as much higher as circumstances may permit." Burr, he said, was trying to "play the game of confusion, and I feel it a religious duty to oppose his career."

A dozen years before the duel at Weehawken, Hamilton was savaging Burr and declaring it a "religious duty" to oppose him. Hamilton was mystified by Burr, a man who seemed to have no fixed allegiances. He saw treachery in the way Burr flirted with both parties and seemed to draw a veil over his own genuine point of view. Burr also posed a threat to Hamilton's political base in New York, and, of course, he had earned Hamilton's enmity by defeating his father-in-law, Philip Schuyler, in the 1791 Senate race. Still—even for the hotheaded Hamilton—such rage at Burr seems over the top.

Hamilton was writing about someone he knew well. They had both served with honor in the Revolution, met in the courtrooms and drawing rooms of New York, broken bread at each other's table. Imagine two men close enough to call each other "Alex" and "Aaron." Theirs had seemed a friendly rivalry—until now. Hamilton's words were tinged with a personal hatred. The thoughts he poured onto paper about Aaron Burr were far more cutting and virulent than anything he ever recorded about Thomas Jefferson. He painted Burr as a soul almost beyond redemption. Something about Burr gnawed at Hamilton, earning him special scorn in Hamilton's pantheon of villains. When Hamilton's friend Gouverneur Morris became minister to Great Britain, Hamilton assigned code names to people so he could write to Morris in confidence. He pointedly gave Burr the code name Savius. The name undoubtedly referred to Plautus Savius, considered one of the most debauched men in Rome, accused of seducing his own son. The reference hinted at the depths of Hamilton's feelings, and the use of code names reveals Hamilton's discretion. When he wrote to someone he didn't know as well, he tempered his language, saying that he had heard things that impugned Burr's integrity, but couldn't vouch for the criticisms. Given the network of friends and acquaintances Burr had built up over the years, though, it seems implausible that Hamilton's highly charged attacks didn't get back to him. If they did, Burr let things slide—for the moment.

In October 1792, at the height of Burr's flirtation with the vice presidency, New York governor George Clinton offered him a position on the New York Supreme Court. It was the move of a seasoned operator. In one stroke he would remove a political competitor, reward Burr for having helped make him governor, and put a highly qualified person on the court. It is tempting to imagine how differently history might have turned out if Burr had accepted the appointment. Burr, however, had no desire to abandon the political fray and don the robes of a judge. He turned down the offer.

In the end, Jefferson and the Republicans could not supplant Adams as vice president. Clinton earned thirty electoral votes, Burr just one—from South Carolina. However, Republican party-building efforts did pay off in the House, where they won a majority. They would use this as a base for their battle against the Federalists during Washington's second term. For years Washington himself had been considered above criticism. Now Jefferson and the Republicans, increasingly frustrated by his support for Hamilton's measures, readied to target him for attack.

Hamilton also had weaknesses that the Republicans could exploit. In suggesting that Burr was "unprincipled" and "not unblemished" in his private life, Alexander Hamilton seemed to be hinting that Burr was a philanderer or guilty of some other act of moral turpitude. It was a surprising and dangerous charge, considering that Hamilton, himself, was entangled in a romantic affair that eventually would explode into the headlines and threaten everything he held dear.

FIVE

SEDUCTION AND STRIFE

Eleven years before

In 1793, the rising star of the Senate, Aaron Burr, moved with his beloved wife and daughter, both named Theodosia, into a luxurious Manhattan mansion known as Richmond Hill. It was a two-story frame house built in the 1750s and situated on 160 acres of land just south of Greenwich Village. Vice President John Adams had made Richmond Hill his official residence a few years before when New York was the nation's seat of government. "In natural beauty it might vie with the most delicious spot I ever saw," wrote Adams's wife Abigail.

The stately formal dining room on the second floor looked out over the Hudson River, just a few hundred feet away. Burr renovated the building from top to bottom, decorating it with elegant imported furnishings. He filled the large library with hundreds of books, and created a window-lined gallery to display his art collection. He lavished attention on the grounds as well, adding an ornamental pond among other touches. Like Washington's Mount Vernon or Jefferson's Monticello, Burr's house became his showplace, an extension of his public image. Here he threw grand parties with many of the most well-known personages of the day in attendance. He also supported promising young artists and writers by putting them up from time to time.

John Adams seemed scandalized when he heard that Burr had moved there. "Is Mr. Burr a man of such ample fortune as to purchase Richmond Hill?" he queried his son Charles, also an attorney in New York. How, Adams wondered, could Burr afford "to make improvements of very expensive kinds? Is the practice of law such a mine of gold?" In fact, Burr could not afford it—his lavish lifestyle and land speculation were pushing him deeper and deeper into a hole of debt that would haunt him for his entire life. He was constantly borrowing money from friends, relatives, and clients. "So hampered by money matters," he wrote to a colleague, "that I am not master of my own time."

To keep the money coming in, he continued practicing law even as he served in the Senate, a fairly common practice at the time. Sometime that year he agreed to represent a twenty-five-year-old woman named Maria Reynolds, who was seeking a divorce from her philandering husband. James Reynolds, she bitterly complained, had abandoned her and her daughter. We don't know exactly how she found her way to Aaron Burr. Reynolds was an attractive blonde who seemed to have easy entrée to a lot of distinguished men in the government. Burr was acquainted with the man she married once the divorce came through, as well as others who knew her, so perhaps that's how it happened. Burr never explained.

He also never let on as to what degree his client confided in him. It is easy to imagine him listening attentively as she poured out her life story in tears. Maria Reynolds regarded herself as wretchedly abused and misused, and she certainly had a sordid tale to tell. It was a story that Burr would have found particularly fascinating, since the central character was someone he knew exceedingly well: Alexander Hamilton.

Maria Reynolds had sought out Hamilton's assistance two years earlier, in July 1791. Hamilton was living with his wife and four children at a red brick home in Philadelphia, still the seat of the federal government. She showed up at the door and asked to speak with him in private, where she spun a tale of woe similar to the one she later told Burr. Her husband had treated her cruelly and left her for another woman. As a fellow New Yorker, she was begging Hamilton for money to enable her to return to New York.

Hamilton could never forget the way his mother had been mistreated and abandoned, so he had a soft spot for women in need. Recently, for example, he had taken up the cause of a widow seeking compensation for her husband's war losses. Hamilton also had a reputation for being a flirt and perhaps something more. He seemed to come alive in the company of women, the contentious politician becoming convivial and playful with ladies present. He made no secret of his appreciation for beautiful women. One congressman found it amusing to observe Hamilton casting lustful glances at other men's wives during a dinner party. A delectable story that made the rounds involved Angelica Schuyler Church, Hamilton's sister-in-law. At a 1789 social gathering, a bow fell off Angelica's shoe. Hamilton, whose wife was not present, acted the part of the dashing gallant, sweeping the bow off the floor. Angelica's younger sister Peggy pinned it on Hamilton's lapel, saying, "There brother, I have made you a knight." When Angelica playfully pretended that he could not be a Knight of the Garter in America, Peggy raised eyebrows with a quick-witted double entendre: "True, sister, but *he would be if you let him.*"

Now Hamilton was face-to-face with an alluring young woman begging for his assistance. He quickly agreed to help. That evening, he brought some cash to the rooming house where she lived. He was shown to her room at the top of the stairs; she invited him in. Hamilton later described what happened next: "Some conversation ensued from which it was quickly apparent that other than pecuniary consolation would be acceptable." He lacked the will to resist, and they quickly fell into bed.

Hamilton started seeing Maria regularly. Shortly after their first assignation, Eliza Hamilton and their four children left to spend the summer at her father's estate in Albany. Once she was safely away, Hamilton began bedding Maria in his own home. When Eliza wrote Hamilton to say she was thinking of coming home early, he encouraged her to stay away longer, allowing him more freedom to keep romancing his mistress. When Eliza and the family returned, he continued to see Maria at her place.

Hamilton was engaging in incredibly risky behavior for such a public figure, and the other shoe dropped in December. It turned out that Maria's husband, James Reynolds, was not a clueless cuckold. He knew all about the affair—in fact, he most likely encouraged it—and now he threw his knowledge in Hamilton's face. Reynolds threatened to expose Hamilton as a philanderer, called him "the cruelest man in existence" for ruining Reynolds's marriage, and asked for a thousand dollars (the equivalent of perhaps $20,000 today) to keep mum. Maria played on Hamilton's heartstrings, begging forgiveness for having brought this to pass: "I wish I had never been born to give you so much unhappiness." Hamilton—understandably rattled about what such a revelation might do to his family and career—paid the hush money.

Incredibly, he kept on seeing Maria. He tried halfheartedly to end the affair, but she pleaded with him to come back. Not only that, but James Reynolds joined the chorus and urged Hamilton to visit their home and consider his wife "a friend." Far from being the injured party, Reynolds was all too happy to play the part of both pimp and extortionist. He continued to encourage Hamilton to see Maria, even as he demanded more money. How someone as shrewd as Hamilton could be so easily manipulated by these two boggles the mind.

He couldn't break away. Maria utterly bewitched him.

"The variety of shapes which this woman could assume was endless," he later confessed. His self-destructive compulsion was matched by his unbelievable naiveté. He desperately continued to hope that Maria harbored genuine affection for him, whereas it seems far more plausible that she was complicit in the blackmail from the outset. After nearly a year entwined with his mistress, it finally dawned on Hamilton the degree of peril he was in, and he broke things off in the summer of 1792. The damage was done, though, as he would soon discover.

James Reynolds was a familiar type, a bottom feeder forever devising schemes to get rich from the government. These included lawsuits, shady speculation, even an attempt to wheedle George Washington into giving him a government job. Then he hooked up with Jacob Clingman, who had clerked for Pennsylvania congressman and soon-to-be Speaker of the House Frederick Muhlenberg. Reynolds and Clingman became partners in crime, hatching a plan to defraud the Treasury Department. Their swindle was discovered a few months after Hamilton broke off the affair, and they were arrested in November 1792.

Clingman had seen Hamilton with Maria on several occasions, and may even have been a party to the blackmail scheme. The Reynoldses had bragged to Clingman about all the money Hamilton had paid them. Eager to evade prosecution, Clingman decided to leverage his connections and his knowledge.

First he convinced his old boss, Congressman Muhlenberg, to go to bat for him. Muhlenberg believed his former clerk was a young man of good character who had been lead astray by Reynolds, who he deemed a "rascal." Muhlenberg helped Clingman get out on bail, and even went so far as to meet with Treasury Secretary Hamilton to see about getting the charges dropped. He brought along a colleague— Senator Aaron Burr. As Hamilton sat in his office conversing with the two men, it is easy to imagine him calculating the dangers the situation posed, and how best to navigate around them. Maintaining a discreet silence about his relationship with Reynolds and Clingman, he indicated he would do what he could to help Muhlenberg's former clerk.

Muhlenberg and Burr eventually brokered a deal allowing Clingman and Reynolds to avoid prison by making restitution. In the weeks that took to negotiate, however, Clingman upped the ante by hinting to Muhlenberg that he had evidence of a scandal involving Hamilton, and that his jailed partner knew even more. It wasn't the cabinet member's titillating sexcapades that Clingman was selling. He suggested something far more insidious. Clingman alleged that Hamilton was feathering his own nest through illegal financial speculation relating to the Treasury, and that he had secretly paid Reynolds as part of the plot. The hints turned into direct accusations. Reynolds, said Clingman, "had it in his power to hang the Secretary of the Treasury."

This was one red-hot potato. It was an article of faith among Republicans that Hamilton was totally corrupt, and using his post at Treasury to enrich himself. One rumor purported that he had shipped $100,000 in ill-gotten gold to Europe for safekeeping. Any proof of such wrongdoing would fatally damage George Washington's administration and possibly end Hamilton's career. Muhlenberg could not ignore Clingman's allegations, but he wanted help looking into them. He recruited two Virginia congressmen to work with him, Abraham Venable and James Monroe. The trio investigated the charges, meeting with Clingman and both James and Maria Reynolds. Hamilton had begged Maria to burn his letters, but instead she gave some of them to the congressmen, confirming that Hamilton had made payoffs to her husband. James Reynolds, still in jail, offered tantalizing promises to blow the whistle on Hamilton when he was freed. Once his release was arranged, however, he bolted.

Everything the investigating congressmen heard supported their suspicions that Hamilton was engaged in nefarious activities that had to be laid before the president. They prepared a letter to George Washington, but offered Hamilton a chance to defend himself before they sent it. Muhlenberg, Venable, and Monroe met at Hamilton's Philadelphia house on December 15, 1792, to hear him out.

Hamilton stunned them with the explanation he put forward. This, he said, was not a case of public wrongdoing, but rather one of private indiscretion. The payments to Reynolds involved not a whiff of official misconduct—they were blackmail. He walked the congressmen through his torrid affair in excruciating detail, to the point that they begged him to stop. Hamilton, however, was incapable of going halfway. He shared love letters from Maria and demands for money from her husband. According to Hamilton, "The result was a full and unequivocal acknowledgement" by the congressmen that they accepted and believed his explanation. That may have been wishful thinking. While Venable and Muhlenberg made profuse apologies for intruding on Hamilton's private life, Hamilton noticed that Monroe remained distinctly chilly. "We left him under the impression our suspicions were removed," wrote Monroe, suggesting that some doubt still lurked in his mind at least. He decided to hold onto the cache of letters that had been entrusted to him.

Alexander Hamilton frequently portrayed himself as a man of unchallenged virtue. A few months after the affair came to an end, he boldly proclaimed in a letter "that the strictest scrutiny into every part of my conduct, whether as a private citizen or as a public officer, can only serve to establish the perfect purity of it." Of course, he knew that was far from the case. Moreover, he knew that others knew. His dalliance with Maria Reynolds was a ticking time bomb waiting to blow up his cherished reputation. For the next few years, as the country lurched through a series of crises and convulsions, he could only hope that it wouldn't blow him sky high.

By the time President Washington's second term began in 1793, Hamilton had expanded the Treasury Department until it occupied an entire block in downtown Philadelphia. He led an army of administrators, accountants, customs inspectors, and surveyors. He battled every day for his vision of America, embracing capitalism, commerce, entrepreneurship, and the Industrial Revolution. All the while, his actions and his prestige were assaulted as more and more public criticism was directed his way. He and Jefferson found themselves "daily pitted in the cabinet like two cocks," as Jefferson recalled. "It was impossible for two men to be of more opposite principles." Jefferson, who planned to leave the cabinet by the end of the year, found himself drowning under the deluge of Hamilton's rhetoric. During one interminable cabinet meeting, Jefferson complained that Hamilton made an inflammatory forty-five-minute speech that sounded like an argument before a jury. Washington grew weary of their battles, but could do little to rein them in. Observing how frequently Washington sided with Hamilton, Jefferson began to murmur that Washington was growing senile, and showed "a willingness to let others act and even think for him." By "others," of course, he meant Hamilton.

The year 1792 had seen the country gripped by a financial panic, precipitated in part by speculation in government bonds. Hamilton's former number two at Treasury, William Duer, turned out to be one of the chief speculators. When the bottom fell out of the market, Duer went to prison and Hamilton's opponents howled that the treasury secretary must have been involved. Finding himself frequently under attack, Hamilton put his pen to work. He would write ten, fifteen, and twenty-part essays, anonymously attacking his opponents. Thomas Jefferson, by contrast, rarely deigned to write such pieces himself, preferring to delegate that task to his attack dogs: political allies such as Madison and Monroe, or friendly editors whose newspapers he subsidized with loans or government jobs.

Jefferson did get personally involved in an effort to have Hamilton censured by Congress. He secretly drew up a series of resolutions calling out the secretary of the treasury for his high-handed running of the Treasury, which he then slipped to Congressman William Giles, who introduced them on the floor of the House. The *National Gazette,* a newspaper published by a Jefferson ally, supported the resolutions, proclaiming that Hamilton "fancies himself the great pivot upon which the whole machine of government turns, throwing out of view...the president, the legislature and the Constitution itself." The anti-Hamilton resolutions were defeated in March 1793, but Hamilton continued to be the target of fierce attacks, a subject he whimsically touched upon in a letter to Angelica Schuyler Church. "You will ask why I do not quit this disagreeable trade," he wrote. "How can I? What is to become of my fame and glory?"

As Hamilton was making more and more enemies, Aaron Burr was making a name for himself in the Senate. Joining the outcry over speculation that had led to the financial panic, he proposed a constitutional amendment that forbade congressmen from holding stock in banks. When Federalists sought to unseat Pennsylvania senator Albert Gallatin, a fierce critic of Hamilton and the Federalists, Burr led his defense. Federalists argued that the Swiss-born Gallatin was a foreign interloper, ineligible to serve because he hadn't been an American citizen for a long enough time. Gallatin was removed from his seat, but Burr's stirring arguments won him renown nonetheless. With an eye toward his political future, Burr cultivated friendships with Virginia Republicans James Madison and James Monroe. Burr's wife Theodosia joined him for a while in Philadelphia, but her health was declining and she couldn't stand the snobbery she found in government circles, so she retreated back to New York. Meanwhile, her husband, like many others in the U.S. government, found his gaze inexorably drawn to the bloody goings-on across the Atlantic. Rage and revenge had taken the reins in France, and the repercussions of the bloodstained convulsions of the French Revolution would dominate American politics for years.

Revolutionaries stormed the Bastille in 1789. By the time of Washington's second inaugural in March of 1793, the guillotine was working overtime. King Louis XVI had lost his head—along with thousands of others—and France was awash in gore. Just a few weeks later, word reached American shores that France and England were going to war. George Washington called a cabinet meeting to decide what the United States would do.

Popular opinion tilted toward France, whose timely military assistance had empowered victory in the American Revolution just a dozen years before. Thomas Jefferson, who had been in Paris during the first heady days of the uprising, was intensely sympathetic to the Revolution. The rallying cry, "Liberty, Equality, Fraternity," resonated strongly with Jefferson, who championed liberty above all things and hated monarchy with a passion. By contrast, Hamilton and many other Federalists were horrified by the bloodshed and fearful that the Revolution was already spawning anarchy and mob rule. They were also sharply influenced by the fact that nine-tenths of all imports came from Great Britain, the country's number one trading partner. Any move to support France over Britain could have a disastrous impact on the fragile United States economy. After a contentious cabinet meeting, Washington issued a Proclamation of Neutrality.

At almost the exact same time, the new French ambassador arrived in Charleston, South Carolina, and set out for Philadelphia. Citizen Genêt, as he was universally known, was thirty years old with flaming red hair and a personality to match. Frenzied crowds greeted him at rallies, banquets, and meetings. Republicans formed political clubs advocating support for France. These clubs were suspected by many Federalists of being breeding grounds for treason and sedition. Genêt demanded the right to outfit privateers against the English. He raised the temperature considerably when he threatened to go over Washington's head and take his appeal to the American people. John Adams was consumed with worry that angry mobs would drag Washington out of his house and bring the violence and chaos of the French Revolution to the streets of Philadelphia. Federalists started calling Republicans "Jacobins," likening them to the most fiercely radical faction in the French Revolution. Republicans, in turn, portrayed the Federalists as monarchists who opposed true liberty and democracy.

Support for France over Great Britain went through the roof when the British refused to respect America's neutrality and seized more than three hundred American merchant ships in the Caribbean to "impress" American seamen, removing them from their vessels and forcing them to serve aboard British ships. A fresh wave of protest erupted across the country. Federalists were appalled at the Crown's heavy-handed conduct that threatened war. "The English are absolute madmen," said Massachusetts congressman Fisher Ames.

President Washington decided to send a special envoy to England to work things out. Hamilton wanted the job, and Washington seemed willing to give it to him. Republicans were apoplectic that the hated Hamilton might be appointed. By this time Jefferson had resigned from the cabinet and returned to Monticello, so it was up to his fellow Republicans to lead the charge. Representative John Nicholas, brother-in-law of James Monroe, sputtered to Washington, "more than half [of] Americans have determined it to be unsafe to trust power in the hands of this person" because of "the many odious traits of his character." The real issue, of course, was Hamilton's unwavering regard for the British government. Washington decided that Hamilton lacked "the general confidence of the country" and dispatched John Jay, the chief justice of the Supreme Court, to England. Aaron Burr led Republican opposition to the appointment. Anticipating later arguments over separation of powers, he argued that it was "contrary to the spirit of the Constitution" that the head of one branch, the judiciary, should be working for the leader of another branch, the executive. Nevertheless, the Senate confirmed Jay along party lines. On May 12, 1794, with thousands of people lining the docks to see him off, Jay sailed for London.

To balance things out, Washington decided that he would replace the minister to France with a Republican sympathetic to the French Revolution. A congressional committee, led by Madison and Monroe, called on President Washington and strongly recommended the appointment of Aaron Burr. Monroe was absolutely convinced that Washington would go along. He was shocked when the president brusquely declared that the appointment of Burr was "out of the question," and instead selected Monroe himself. Washington claimed that he didn't want to replace the incumbent minister with another New Yorker. It seems far more plausible that it stemmed from the longstanding hostility Washington and Hamilton felt for Burr, whose character they both had questioned. It could also have been a matter of jealousy—Hamilton may have been determined to keep Burr from a foreign post when he could not have one himself.

In any case, it was a severe blow to Burr, the second calamity to befall him in little more than a week. Ten days earlier, his wife Theodosia had died at age forty-seven after a long and debilitating illness.

They had been married for twelve years. She was the great love of his life, "the woman whose life brought me more happiness than all my success, and whose death has dealt me more pain than all sorrows combined." He would never love another the way he did Theodosia.

To fill the hole in his heart, Burr turned his attentions to his eleven-year-old daughter, also named Theodosia. He was a feminist of sorts. In fact, when Mary Wollstonecraft published her provocative *A Vindication of the Rights of Women* in 1792, considered the first great feminist treatise, Burr wrote to his wife, "Be assured that your sex has in her an able advocate...I promise myself much pleasure in reading it to you." Now Burr resolved to engage in a "fair experiment" to educate his daughter in a way few women of the time were. In other words, to educate her as if she had been a son. He devoted an immense amount of energy to this endeavor. He was frequently away, so he tutored her by mail, asking questions and correcting her answers. When she reached adulthood, Theodosia became one of her father's closest confidantes.

As if the upheaval in France wasn't crisis enough for the Washington administration, a simmering conflict in western Pennsylvania erupted into open rebellion in the summer of 1794. Thousands of farmers threatened to march on Pittsburgh, and execution of public officials was seriously proposed. It all happened over whiskey.

Back in 1791, searching for desperately needed sources of revenue for the federal government, Alexander Hamilton hit upon the idea of taxing distilled spirits. Congress went along, and the tax was introduced into law. Few in Congress opposed it, but one who did was

Pennsylvania senator William Maclay. He prophetically predicted that once the law went into effect, "War and bloodshed are the most likely consequences."

Farmers in western Pennsylvania who distilled their surplus corn into whiskey were outraged by the new tax. How could the far-off federal government impose a tax on them? Treasury officials sent to enforce the law were tarred and feathered. Mass meetings threatened further violence. Many of the protestors were veterans of the Revolution, who compared the whiskey tax to the British taxes that sparked the American rebellion.

Alexander Hamilton urged President Washington to take decisive action. Hesitant to take up arms against his fellow citizens, Washington tried to cool things down by other means. Matters came to a head in August 1794, when six thousand rebels mustered an army to oppose the tax. Their leaders proposed building guillotines and attacking a government garrison in Pittsburgh to appropriate weapons for their rebellion. Hamilton exhorted Washington to literally assume the mantle of commander-in-chief and lead an overwhelming force of twelve thousand men into Pennsylvania to put down the revolt: "Whenever the government appears in arms it ought to appear like a *Hercules* and inspire respect by the display of strength."

After the rebellious farmers refused an order to disband, Washington determined that he had to take action. "If the laws are to be trampled upon with impunity," he explained, "and a minority is to dictate to the majority, there is an end put at one stroke to Republican Government." He personally took command of a force composed of militia units from Virginia, Maryland, New Jersey, and Pennsylvania itself. Washington led his troops into western Pennsylvania—ironically, the scene of his first military experience in the French and Indian War nearly four decades earlier. With Secretary of War Henry Knox away in Maine, Alexander Hamilton acted as Washington's second-in-command. The two old comrades were in the field again. Republican newspapers carped that Hamilton was once more indulging his insatiable quest for power.

Once the army reached the western part of the state, the rebellion all but dissolved. As Hamilton wrote with satisfaction to his sister-in-law Angelica, "a large army has cooled the courage of those madmen." Dozens of leaders were arrested and jailed, but all were later pardoned or acquitted. Predictably, Federalists and Republicans differed in their reactions. Federalists cheered the government for upholding the laws. Republicans jeered the increasing concentration of power in the hands of the executive branch.

Hamilton had worked tirelessly to help put down what became known as the Whiskey Rebellion. Returning to Philadelphia in December 1794, he told Washington he was going to resign. He was exhausted after four months in the field, and four years of being badgered by his enemies while serving as secretary of the treasury. He could point to tremendous accomplishments. The Treasury Department, which did not even exist when he took office, was now a thriving concern, as was the National Bank that he had created. Washington wrote Hamilton a warm letter extolling his virtues, saying, "My confidence in your talents, exertions, and integrity has been well placed." From London, Angelica Schuyler Church bemoaned Hamilton's departure. "The country will lose one of her best friends," she wrote him plaintively.

The country was on a firm financial footing—which was more than could be said for Hamilton himself. "I am not worth exceeding five hundred dollars in the world," he mused ruefully. "My slender fortune and the best years of my life have been devoted to the service of my adopted country." So much for charges that Hamilton enriched himself in office. Now it was time for him to return to his law practice in New York, replenish his coffers, and see what the future held.

Hamilton returned to New York just as another gubernatorial race was shaping up. Aaron Burr threw his hat in the ring again, repeating his strategy of appealing to both Federalists and Republicans. With everyone taking sides, it was a questionable approach. One Federalist claimed to oppose Burr "not because I know him to belong to either one faction or another, but because I believe him to belong to none." Burr seemed to be building his own party, loosely allied with the Republicans but loyal only to himself.

During this campaign Burr began to demonstrate his growing abilities as a political organizer. Rather than delegate the nuts and bolts of his campaign to someone else, he was willing to get his own hands dirty, gathering information and winning over voters in person. This was highly unusual at the time, when candidates often portrayed themselves as disinterested parties. Burr did not see the need to cloak his aspirations. His willingness to take to the campaign trail gave ammunition to critics who attacked his ambition. Noah Webster, editor of the Federalist newspaper *American Minerva* (and future dictionary compiler), mocked Burr when he wrote about "a certain little Senator, running about the streets, whispering soft things in people's ears, and making large entertainments."

Burr eventually withdrew his candidacy before the election, when he saw that he was not going to have a serious chance. Even so, he had gained some traction. The race for governor had helped him build his base and hone his skills as a political operative. He would pit those skills against Alexander Hamilton and the Federalists to great effect in the years to come.

The country was thrown into a new uproar in 1795 over the treaty that John Jay negotiated with England. True, Jay had secured neutrality and avoided war. Yet it seemed to many that he had caved on everything else, and come back with a very one-sided deal. Even many Federalists were privately appalled.

George Washington was so alarmed that he demanded the Senate consider the treaty in secret. Aaron Burr opposed the secrecy. He wrote to Washington asking for a meeting to discuss it. Washington would not even respond. Burr made a powerful speech opposing the treaty, but it passed along party lines.

When it was made public in July 1795, it tore the country apart. George Washington wrote: "the cry against the Treaty is like that against a mad dog; and every one, in a manner, seems engaged in running it down." Jay said that he could travel across the country at night by the light of fires where he was being burned in effigy. An unknown graffiti artist chalked a graphic sign on the walls of a building near his New York City home:

Damn John Jay. Damn everyone who won't damn John Jay. Damn everyone that won't put up lights in the windows and sit up all night damning John Jay.

Saturday, July 18, 1795, saw an extraordinary spectacle unfold on the streets of Manhattan. Thousands of angry treaty opponents demonstrated at Federal Hall. When Alexander Hamilton tried to organize a counter-demonstration, the crowd shouted him down and stoned him. Blood flowed from a wound in his forehead. Arguments, shouting matches, and fistfights erupted all over the city.

Hamilton whipped himself into a state of hysteria reminiscent of the battlefield rage he exhibited at Monmouth Courthouse. Careening from one knot of people to another, he seemed almost out of control. Coming upon several members of the Livingston family, his political opponents, he put up his fists and declared he was ready to fight the "whole detestable faction" one by one. He challenged two people to duels within two hours. The challenges were serious enough that Hamilton wrote out a will as he prepared to defend his honor. The duels were eventually averted by seconds who negotiated apologies deemed sufficient by Hamilton. Honor had again been preserved without resorting to bloodshed.

Stepping back from the street battles, Hamilton took up his pen to defend the treaty, authoring twenty-eight essays. Reading them at Monticello, his mountaintop retreat, Thomas Jefferson paid Hamilton the highest of compliments. "Hamilton is really a colossus to the anti-republican party. Without numbers, he is a host within himself." In other words, he was a mighty army of one that had to be reckoned with.

Over the past seven years, battles over the Constitution, Hamilton's financial plan, relations with France, and the whiskey tax had transformed the American political landscape. The Jay Treaty was the last step of this massive upheaval. The crucible of American politics had forged loose coalitions into hard and fast political parties. In 1796, these two swords of fire-tempered steel would clash and clang in America's first two-party presidential election.

★ ★ ★

Vice President John Adams would be the Federalist candidate for president. South Carolinian Thomas Pinckney, recently returned home after a stint as minister to Great Britain, would stand for vice president. A Republican congressional caucus selected Thomas Jefferson as their presidential candidate, and Aaron Burr for vice president.

Two tickets. It seemed simple enough. In practice, it was more of a free-for-all. Electors each voted for two candidates. The top vote getter became president. So, in essence, it was a four-way race. That led to all sorts of wild scheming and machinations. Electors contemplated how to use their second vote to thwart the plans of the candidate they hated the most.

Hamilton preferred Pinckney over Adams, who he thought lacked the temperament to succeed Washington. His number one goal, though, was to keep Jefferson out. "All personal and partial considerations must be discarded," he argued, "and every thing must give way to the great object of excluding Jefferson." Hamilton gingerly advocated for Pinckney before grudgingly throwing his support to Adams.

Meantime, some Republicans were uneasy about their own their vice-presidential candidate. The year before, James Monroe, still serving as minister to France, wrote Thomas Jefferson a coded message about Burr. Something had been whispered in Monroe's ear that turned him against his supposed friend and ally. "I consider Burr as a man to be shunned...he is an unprincipled adventurer and whom it is better to get rid of at once. Can you promote this object?"

Blissfully unaware of Monroe's transatlantic barbs, Burr began laying the foundations of his campaign in 1795. He traveled first to New

England and Virginia to seek support. He journeyed to Monticello to confer privately with Jefferson, who apparently disregarded Monroe's warning. Other Republicans, however, had qualms about Burr in line with Monroe's trepidation. One Virginia Republican mused that Burr "has an unequalled talent for attaching men to his view, and forming combinations of which he is always in the center," while seeming to be more interested in mouthing the party line than actually putting it into effect. Federalist Theodore Sedgwick, a friend of Burr's and a man with great political insight, predicted that southern Republicans would not vote for Burr. "Although they covet the aid of his character & talents, they have not the smallest confidence in his hearty union to their cause," wrote Sedgwick. "They doubtless respect Burr's talents, but they dread his independence of them."

That September, in the midst of the campaign, President Washington issued his Farewell Address. Alexander Hamilton had been instrumental in drafting it. The address was not just a nostalgic farewell, it was a six-thousand-word civics lesson packed with observations and warnings that had a distinctly Hamiltonian ring. Published in numerous newspapers, it called for Americans to abhor political parties, cherish public credit, embrace neutrality, and above all, frown upon "every attempt to alienate any portion of our country from the rest, or to enfeeble the sacred ties which now link together the various parts." It immediately became a political football. Republican editor William Duane summarily dismissed Washington's remarks as the "loathings of a sick mind." Washington had once been regarded as untouchable, the untainted hero, a man above politics. It is a measure of how vastly things had changed that revolutionary firebrand Thomas Paine, the author of "Common Sense," felt moved to write an open letter expressing the hope that Washington would drop dead, adding caustically, "the world will be puzzled to decide whether you . . . have abandoned good principles or whether you ever had any."

Burr threw himself vigorously into the presidential campaign. In October, Republican operative John Beckley informed Jefferson ally James Madison that "Burr has been out electioneering these six weeks." Beckley was also suspicious, concluding that Burr was campaigning more for himself than for the party, and wondered if it would be prudent to have some Virginia electors vote against him. The concern, of course, was that, in this topsy-turvy race, Burr might end up with more votes than Jefferson.

In the end, John Adams beat Thomas Jefferson by three electoral votes. The impetuous Adams blamed Hamilton's maneuverings for his narrow margin, and never forgave him. Adams wrote his wife Abigail that Hamilton was "as great an hypocrite as any in the U.S. His intrigues in the election I despise." His response, he declared, would be to keep Hamilton at arm's length.

Despite his energetic campaigning, Burr received only thirty electoral votes, the least among the four major candidates. Most southern electors who voted for Jefferson did not support his vice-presidential candidate. Burr believed that he had been promised the votes of the Virginia electors, but after voting for Jefferson, most of them threw away their second vote on Samuel Adams, who wasn't even running. "The event will not a little mortify Burr," crowed Hamilton when he heard. "Virginia has given him only one Vote." The Philadelphia *Gazette of the United States,* a Federalist paper, piled on with even more mockery. "If a man sticks to his party like a Burr, even Virginia will sooner vote for old Scratch, than for him." Burr felt angry and ill used by the Virginians, but in typical Burr fashion, he nursed his grievances quietly.

The 1796 election was over. Feisty Federalist John Adams would be president, but the party's most aggressive activist, Alexander Hamilton, was on the outs. Since the Federalists had captured the New York legislature, Aaron Burr would lose his Senate seat. There was speculation that his humiliating showing as a candidate for vice president, coupled with being forced from the Senate, might prove the end of his career. Both Hamilton and Burr would be searching for a way to be relevant, and they would be jostling elbows in the crowded cockpit of New York City. Unbeknownst to either, the Maria Reynolds time bomb was about to go off. The scandalous blast would fling them together in the strangest of ways, and open the door for an unexpected alliance between the two men.

FOUR

FRIENDS OR ENEMIES

Seven years before

On Tuesday morning, July 11, 1797, Hamilton was trembling with rage. The target of his anger was future president James Monroe, who had just returned from Europe upon being recalled as minister to France. When Hamilton accused Monroe of being a liar, the Virginian became equally incensed. The two men leapt out of their chairs and began screaming at each other.

"Do you say I represented falsely? You are a scoundrel!" Monroe shouted.

"I will meet you like a gentleman," Hamilton fired back.

"I am ready. Get your pistols!" Monroe retorted.

The subject of the angry confrontation was the Maria Reynolds affair. The exchange took place seven years *to the day* before the duel in Weehawken. Ironically, it would be up to none other than Aaron Burr to make sure it did not lead to bloodshed.

★ ★ ★

James Callender was a Republican-leaning journalist with a reputation as a hack and a scandalmonger who specialized in rabidly partisan hatchet jobs. Thomas Jefferson encouraged him, subsidized him, praised him as a "man of genius," and then, once Jefferson became president, dropped him like a hot potato. At which point Callender retaliated against his onetime sponsor by accusing him in print of having fathered multiple children with one of his slaves, Sally Hemmings—charges which many discounted as sour grapes at the time, but which most historians today regard as true.

In June 1797, Callender published a pamphlet publicly exposing Hamilton's affair with Maria Reynolds. For good measure, he also printed the trove of sensitive letters that James Monroe had held for safekeeping. "So much correspondence could not refer exclusively to wenching," argued Callender. He jumped to the same conclusion that Monroe and the other two congressmen had initially reached six years earlier. Hamilton, he proclaimed, could not have been stupid enough to pay hush money for sex; therefore, Hamilton's payments to Reynolds must be evidence of corruption and wrongdoing.

Hamilton decided that the only way to respond was to rip the cover off his private life, to sacrifice his reputation in order to preserve his honor. He published an astounding ninety-five-page booklet that freely confessed his philandering, but emphatically denied the accusations of corruption. "The charge against me is a connection with one James Reynolds for purposes of improper pecuniary speculation," he wrote. "My real crime is an amorous connection with his wife, for a considerable time with his…connivance…with the design to extort money from me." He overwhelmed readers with titillating details, while self-righteously portraying himself as a man of upright principles under attack from enemies who wanted to destroy him.

The country was thunderstruck by his revelations. Rumors about the affair had circulated in Philadelphia and New York, but now Hamilton had confirmed them in excruciating detail. The Republican press had a field day. Callender himself bubbled over with joy in a letter he wrote to Jefferson: "If you have not seen it, no anticipation can equal the infamy of this piece." Callender wrote mockingly that Hamilton's arguments could be boiled down to this: "I am a rake and for that reason cannot be a swindler." Jefferson and many other Republicans, disbelieving Hamilton's protestations, continued to believe he was both.

Modern commentators often spout this adage about the damage done by political scandals: "It's not the crime, it's the cover-up." Hamilton would seem the exception to this rule, inflicting a severe wound on himself with his excessive and almost compulsive explanations, combined with a pose of injured innocence that many found infuriating. After reading the pamphlet, Hamilton's former ally James Madison shook his head at what he called "a curious specimen of the ingenious folly of its author." Repulsed by the rhetorical excess, Madison remarked to Thomas Jefferson that Hamilton was "forgetting that simplicity and candor are the only dress which prudence would put on innocence."

Hamilton was the Republicans' great bête noire, the corrupt monarchist in bed with conniving speculators who sought to enrich themselves at the expense of hardworking farmers and artisans, suppress democracy, and run the country without interference. What we see today as his signature accomplishments, they viewed as blemishes on the purity of the new nation. Now this self-proclaimed tower of virtue had been brought low by his own indiscretions and his own pen, which had been used so often to rip Republicans to shreds. For Hamilton's enemies, the irony was sweet.

Hamilton's stunned wife Eliza, pregnant for the sixth time, found that her husband's sexual escapades were the talk of the town. His public confession must have been a nightmare for a woman who naturally shied away from the spotlight. At the same time, she was outraged at the attackers who had brought her husband low. She stood by her man. Her sister Angelica wrote a consoling note. "Tranquilize your kind and dear heart," she advised. "Merit, virtue, and talents must have enemies and are always exposed to envy." Eliza could have avoided the nightmare of such attacks, wrote Angelica, only if she had "married into a family less *near the sun*. But then you would have missed the pride, the pleasure, the nameless satisfactions." Eliza burned all of her correspondence, so it is impossible to know what degree of consolation she was able to take from her sister's words.

Hamilton's dirty little secret was on everyone's lips. He was the butt of ribald jests and charges of corruption that threatened his career. Looking for someone to blame, he fixed on James Monroe. Hamilton was convinced that Monroe had leaked the papers to Callender. The timing was certainly suspicious: Callender's incendiary story came out shortly after Monroe returned to the United States. Monroe had motive aplenty: anger at George Washington (and by extension, Hamilton) for recalling him as minister to France, allegedly because Monroe was too cozy with the French.

Hamilton sought a meeting with Monroe, who was visiting family in New York. Monroe heatedly denied Hamilton's accusations. He said he had left the papers "with a friend" (presumably Thomas Jefferson), and professed himself innocent of any knowledge of how they had found their way into James Callender's eager hands. Hamilton didn't believe him, and soon they had to be pulled apart like a pair of snarling pit bulls. A wrathful exchange of letters followed their meetings and Monroe believed that he had been challenged to a duel. He accepted—and then sent Aaron Burr the correspondence and asked him to act as an intermediary.

Two years before, Monroe had called Burr "a man to be shunned." The year before that, Hamilton called him "unprincipled both as a public and private man." Now both their lives were in his hands. Burr was severely ill at the time, but he went right to work trying to defuse the situation. He sought an immediate meeting with Hamilton. Afterwards he scribbled an optimistic note to Monroe: "The thing *will* take an amicable course and terminate, I believe to your satisfaction." Nevertheless, the affair dragged on. Monroe and Hamilton continued to goad each other with letters that Burr called "childish." Burr counseled patience. He withheld some of Monroe's most antagonistic letters, and toned down others. Thanks to his deftness as an intermediary, the whole dispute petered out by the end of the year. It is noteworthy that after representing Maria Reynolds in her divorce, and James Monroe in his dispute with Hamilton, Burr—unlike many other Republicans—was utterly convinced that Hamilton was innocent of the speculation charges. Burr's even-handed treatment of the matter undoubtedly made a powerful impression on Hamilton.

Callender's revelations, coupled with Hamilton's own confession—the "Reynolds Pamphlet," as it came to be known—seriously tarnished Hamilton's reputation. He had tarred himself as an adulterer, but failed to erase suspicions that he had misused his office. Many Federalists worried that one of their most gifted leaders was irrevocably compromised, and would never be able to hold a high post in government again. Massachusetts Federalist David Cobb, more cynical and perhaps more prescient than some of his colleagues, disagreed. "Hamilton is fallen for the present," he wrote. "But if he fornicates with every female in the cities of New York and Philadelphia, he will rise again. For purity of character...is not necessary for public patronage."

Hamilton's affair branded him as a womanizer, a stain that has endured for centuries. Was he really a Casanova who jumped from bed to bed? Benjamin Latrobe, who became architect of the Capitol during the Jefferson administration, labeled Hamilton an "insatiable libertine." John Adams agreed. "His fornications, adulteries and incests [a reference to his alleged affair with his sister-in-law] were propagated far and wide." But these comments came years after the Reynolds affair had been made public, and the men who made them were far from dispassionate about Hamilton. There is, in fact, no convincing evidence that he had an affair with Angelica Schuyler Church or anyone else, aside from Maria Reynolds. Republican editors hostile to Hamilton would have been more than happy to publish any dirt on him they could dig up—reports of illegitimate children or liaisons with other women—but there wasn't any. Hamilton's solicitous letters to his wife in the ensuing years suggest a guilt that he could never quite shake. "I always feel how necessary you are to me," he wrote the following year when she left New York to visit family. "But when you are absent, I become still more sensible of it."

Aaron Burr developed his own reputation as a lothario, especially after the death of his wife in 1794. His friend and biographer Matthew Livingston Davis was scandalized to discover that Burr had collected a "mass of letters" from many female correspondents, indicating "no strict morality on their part," as he delicately put it. Burr insisted on preserving the letters during his lifetime, but Davis burned them on upon his death. Burr occasionally made humorous references to his paramours in letters to his grown daughter. He sometimes shared names from his little black book in letters to friends, and then jocularly pestered them about whether they had followed up. His reputation in this department seems very well deserved.

America's policy of neutrality in the war between England and France was proving difficult to maintain. France responded to the Jay Treaty by severing normal diplomatic ties and sending armed privateers to seize American ships trading with British ports. One armed French vessel snatched several American ships right outside of New York harbor. Public opinion swung against France, and war seemed a distinct possibility. President John Adams sent a special negotiating team to France to find a solution. They sought a meeting with Minister of Foreign Affairs Charles Maurice de Talleyrand-Périgord, famous as a high prince of corruption. Talleyrand dispatched three of his minions, whom the Americans referred to in their dispatches as Messrs. X, Y, and Z. They demanded that the American emissaries fork over a $250,000 bribe. The Americans were outraged. Charles Cotesworth Pinckney of South Carolina shouted, "No, No, No. Not a sixpence!" He and his fellow envoys left France without ever opening formal negotiations.

News of the so-called "XYZ Affair" broke in the spring of 1798, driving the American public into a rage against their former ally. South Carolina congressman Robert Goodloe Harper reshaped Pinckney's response into a rallying cry for war. "Millions for defense, but not one cent for tribute!" Congress rescinded all treaties with France, and passed legislation calling for President Adams to raise a ten-thousand-man "Provisional Army." American naval vessels were given hunting licenses to attack French ships, and soon they were exchanging cannon fire at sea. The conflict became known as the "Quasi War," because the simmering conflict never quite erupted into full-fledged warfare.

President Adams appointed George Washington, then in retirement at Mount Vernon, as commander of the army. Washington reluctantly agreed to accept the position, but only if Adams would name Hamilton as his second-in-command. Adams had come to loathe Hamilton. He considered his fellow Federalist vain, flamboyant, and conniving. He had not forgiven Hamilton for what he deemed a betrayal during the presidential election. The Reynolds affair had convinced the puritanical Adams that Hamilton was a man of debauched morals. He could never get over Hamilton's illegitimate birth in the West Indies, referring to him more than once as a "Creole bastard." Hamilton was the last person he wanted to make Washington's second-in-command. What's more, Hamilton had only served as a colonel during the Revolution, and Adams couldn't see why he should promote him over others who had commanded large bodies of troops as generals.

Washington insisted. He wrote Adams an extraordinary letter extolling Hamilton's leadership abilities. During the Revolution, he said, Hamilton had acted as his chief of staff, and thus understood many things that people who commanded brigades and divisions didn't know. As to his personal qualities: "By some he is considered as an ambitious man, and therefore a dangerous one. That he is ambitious I shall readily grant, but it is of that laudable kind which prompts a man to excel in whatever he takes in hand." Washington went on to call Hamilton enterprising, perceptive, and a man of good judgment—words that must have grated on Adams—and told the president that if he wasn't appointed, "his loss will be irreparable."

Adams got the message. Hamilton got the job. His appointment drew many a snide comment from the Republican press, who referred to him as the "amorous general." It also became the backdrop for a growing rapprochement between Alexander Hamilton and Aaron Burr.

As war fever swept across the United States in June 1798, Hamilton and Burr served together on a military committee organized by the citizens of New York to strengthen the defenses of New York harbor. Mutual acquaintances noted a difference in their interactions after Burr mediated Hamilton's dispute with Monroe. The two men were openly friendly, and Burr was "particularly courteous to Hamilton." Burr was zealous in advocating measures to defend the harbor, a position that surprised Federalists, since many Republicans continued to look favorably on the French and oppose any kind of military buildup. Once again, Burr was going his own way. He worked closely with Hamilton, securing money for the fortifications.

This was just the beginning. Burr was interested in an appointment as the army's quartermaster general. Hamilton was well aware that Burr was heavily in debt—he had recently sold most of his possessions to pay his ballooning bills—and the position of quartermaster general was one with many opportunities for corruption. Given their history, Hamilton might have opposed the appointment for fear that

Burr would abuse it. Instead, he offered to help Burr. When Burr set out for Philadelphia to lobby for the appointment, Hamilton wrote to Treasury Secretary Oliver Wolcott Jr. asking that Burr's request be given serious consideration.

"Colonel Burr sets out today for Philadelphia. I have some reasons for wishing that the administration may manifest a cordiality to him. It is not impossible he will be found a useful cooperator. I am aware there are different sides but the case is worth the experiment." Not exactly a wholehearted endorsement, but quite a turnabout from the presidential election two years earlier.

President Adams was willing. Having such a prominent Republican as a general would lend a bipartisan air to the military buildup. The stumbling block was Washington. "By all that I have known and heard Colonel Burr is a brave and able officer," responded Washington when Adams broached the subject of Burr's appointment, "but the question is whether he has not equal talents at intrigue." Washington's response triggered Adams's wrath. How could Washington reject Burr as an "intriguer" after he had forced Adams to appoint Hamilton, "the most restless, impatient, artful, indefatigable and unprincipled intriguer in the United States, if not in the world, to be second in command"? Secretary of State Timothy Pickering took note of the rejection. "It is impossible that Gen. Washington should confide in him, and therefore he cannot be appointed."

Once again, Washington's antipathy had thwarted Burr's ambition. Of course, Burr reciprocated Washington's disdain. He told Adams he "despised Washington as a man of no talents and one who could not spell a sentence of common English." History might have turned out differently had Burr been appointed quartermaster general, and worked hand in hand with Hamilton to raise the army. Years later, John Adams himself wondered about that. "What would have been the consequence? Shall I say that Hamilton would have been now alive? And Hamilton and Burr now at the head of our affairs? What then?!!!" The president's sage hindsight is something to ponder.

Alexander Hamilton, however, wasn't done boosting Burr's fortunes. He suggested to New York governor John Jay that Burr be given the job of supervising the fortifications being installed at New York. Aware of Burr's financial problems, he added that Burr would require "adequate compensation" to undertake it. Nothing came of this idea, but it was another sign of how much their relationship had warmed.

Hamilton also believed that Burr was coming around to his political point of view. General James Wilkinson, now third in rank behind Hamilton, came to New York to consult with his superior. He mentioned that he was planning to meet with Burr as well. "Little Burr!" exclaimed Hamilton, with apparent affection. "We have always been opposed in politics but always on good terms. We set out in the practice of the law at the same time, and took opposite political directions. Burr beckoned me to follow him, and I advised him to come with me; we could not agree, but I fancy he now begins to think he was wrong and I was right." Whether or not that was true remained to be seen.

As the Adams administration prepared for the possibility of war with France, Federalists in Congress passed a series of repugnant laws that were to prove the party's undoing: the Alien and Sedition Acts.

The country was racked with unrest. A majority of people supported the war measures, but a sizable Republican minority opposed them. Federalists began identifying themselves by decorating their hats with black cockades, while Republicans wore the French tricolors. Protest meetings led to violent street clashes across America, and even spread into the House of Representatives. Republican Matthew Lyon of Vermont and Federalist Roger Griswold of Connecticut had to be pulled apart as they used cane and fist to pummel each other. There was talk of domestic rebellion, even secession.

Increasingly, the Federalists interpreted dissent as treason. They believed French immigrants who had fled to the United States in the aftermath of their Revolution were provoking the violence. As always, fear of anarchy lurked just below the surface. They were convinced that only drastic action could ensure the survival of the government. In addition to making it easier for the Adams administration to deport French immigrants suspected of being spies and provocateurs, the Alien and Sedition Acts made it a crime to publish "any false, scandalous or malicious" attacks on the government, or anything that would bring the government or Congress "into contempt or disrepute." In other words, the laws criminalized criticism.

President John Adams signed the acts into law. Soon, trumped-up charges were being brought against Republican editors and others who opposed the government. Congressman Lyon was jailed for criticizing the president's "unbounded thirst for ridiculous pomp." Alexander Hamilton, who embraced the new laws, must have felt some measure of satisfaction when editor James Callender, who had made the Reynolds affair front-page news, was jailed for nine months.

Federalist zeal for prosecuting critics of the president or the government knew no bounds. The most ridiculous case of overreach involved a couple of men in Newark, New Jersey, who were part of a crowd celebrating the arrival of President John Adams. The two were a bit rambunctious after downing drinks in a nearby tavern and were greatly amused by the spectacle of the sixteen-gun salute fired as the president's carriage rode by.

"There goes the President, and they are firing at his ass," bellowed Brown Clark.

"I don't care if they fire *through* his ass!" responded his drinking companion, Luther Baldwin. Incredibly, both men received jail time and fines as a result of those remarks.

Republicans, naturally appalled, labeled the laws "a most detestable thing." Thomas Jefferson and James Madison secretly drafted fiery resolutions passed by state legislatures in Virginia and Kentucky opposing the Alien and Sedition Acts and warning that they would lead to "revolution and blood." Jefferson believed the laws would ultimately hurt the Federalists. He was confident that in time "we shall see the reign of witches pass over, their spells dissolved, and the people recovering their true sight, restoring the government to its true principles."

The anti-immigrant sentiment that spawned the Alien and Sedition Acts manifested itself in other ways, too. In 1799, Federalists in the New York General Assembly proposed a constitutional amendment to bar foreign-born citizens from holding elective office. Aaron Burr opposed it, giving one of the most passionate speeches of his career. He pointed out that many foreign-born citizens (including Alexander Hamilton, although he didn't mention him) had served in high posts with honor. "America stood with open arms and presented an asylum to the oppressed of every nation," he said. "Shall we deprive these persons of an important right derived from so sacred a source as our Constitution?" It is ironic that it was the native-born Burr, not the immigrant Hamilton, who stood up for citizens who were foreign-born. His speech was in line with his party's opposition to the Adams administration's actions, yet the power of his words suggests that this represented not simply political expediency but a deeply held belief.

Money problems were weighing ever more heavily on Burr. Land speculation, a lavish lifestyle, and efforts to bail out several friends had left him deeply in debt. One deal that went spectacularly bad left him owing $80,000 (roughly equivalent to $2 million today) to a client of Alexander Hamilton's. He was living under threat of financial ruin, which may have motivated what came next: a complicated scheme that would cost him his seat in the legislature and severely damage his fragile new alliance with Hamilton.

It involved drinking water. Or at least it appeared to. New York City had been ravaged by a yellow fever epidemic in 1798. The mosquito-borne disease hollowed out the city, killing upwards of forty people every day. More than two thousand lost their lives. Many blamed the yellow fever outbreak on the city's drinking water, which had been brackish and polluted for years. Aaron Burr proposed creating a privately run water company to bring fresh water from the Bronx River to the city. To carry out this plan, he needed cooperation from the city and a charter from the New York State General Assembly. He solicited a bipartisan group of citizens to help persuade city officials and lawmakers to back the effort. One of those who agreed to help was Alexander Hamilton.

Hamilton at this time was toiling around the clock to bring the Provisional Army into being. He made frequent trips to Scotch Plains, New Jersey, where the new army was drilling. He also corresponded frequently with members of President Adams's cabinet, who consulted him on a variety of issues. He squeezed in work on his law practice when he could, and spent whatever hours were left scribbling essays in support of Federalist policies. His father-in-law, Philip Schuyler, worried that all the work was killing him. "You must make some sacrifice to that health which is so precious to all who are dear to you," he wrote Hamilton, "and to that country which reveres and esteems you." Busy as he was, Hamilton decided to make time to help Burr in what seemed like a worthwhile effort. Burr also offered a quid pro quo: a seat on the board for Hamilton's brother-in-law, John Barker Church, recently returned from Europe with his wife Angelica. Hamilton had a close relationship with Church, a wealthy entrepreneur whom he described as "a man of fortune and integrity—of strong mind, very exact, very active and very much a man of business."

Hamilton lobbied energetically for the project. He joined Burr in a meeting with the mayor of New York, and put his pen to work (as usual) to lay out compelling arguments why such a company would benefit New York. City officials got behind the plan, and as the final days of the legislative session ticked down in March 1799, Burr persuaded his fellow lawmakers to charter the Manhattan Company as a New York corporation.

In truth, though, the idea of a water company to benefit the public was just a ploy. Burr had something else in mind: he wanted to create a bank. New York City had only two banks at the time, and Federalists controlled both of them. Burr wanted to break that monopoly. Many Republicans felt they were at a disadvantage in getting loans. Burr himself, so deeply in debt, would find it immeasurably helpful to have a friendly financial institution backing him up. A Republican-controlled bank would have a political dimension as well. In this era, men could not vote unless they owned property. A bank could offer mortgages, enabling Republicans to add their partisans to the voting rolls. Burr, though, knew that if he openly sought a charter for a Republican-controlled bank, the Federalists in the legislature would shoot it down. So he resorted to some political chicanery.

The water company was a Trojan horse with a bank hidden inside. Just before the bill for the water company was brought to the floor of the New York General Assembly, Burr snuck in a clause saying it was lawful for the company to "employ all such surplus capital" in purchasing stock or "other monied transactions." That single clause gave the Manhattan Company widespread latitude to engage in banking, real estate, and trading.

When the ruse became public, there was an uproar. Burr's actions were seen as incredibly self-serving, and Federalists had no trouble getting the Republican legislators from Manhattan voted out in the next election. Nonetheless, the deal was done.

Stock in the company sold out in a single day, and the board of directors—three-quarters of whom were Republicans—rapidly funneled the bulk of their money into a bank. The water project was downgraded. They abandoned ambitious plans to bring water from the Bronx River, and instead constructed an inadequate system to bring water from nearby wells.

Hamilton had been duped. He understood that Burr had manipulated him with ease, and marveled at what he saw as Burr's hypocrisy. "I have been present when he has contended against banking systems with earnestness & with the same arguments that Jefferson would use," he wrote to a Federalist congressman, yet "he has lately by a trick established a Bank, a perfect monster in its principles; but a very convenient instrument of profit & influence."

The Manhattan Company opened a bank at 40 Wall Street on September 1, 1799. It proved highly successful, growing into the international banking powerhouse Chase Manhattan, which became JPMorgan Chase. The company's water business was quietly shelved for a few decades, but for more than a century the bank had a water committee that met once a year, and reported to the board of directors (presumably with a straight face) that no application for a supply of water had been denied that year.

The bank business was probably enough to dispel any positive feelings Hamilton had developed for Burr. Then, that summer, Burr made it personal: he challenged Hamilton's brother-in-law, John Barker Church, to a duel.

The *casus belli* dated back to when Burr was still in the legislature. He had been approached by a group of European speculators, the Holland Company, which had bought up millions of acres of land in upstate New York. They wanted to change New York laws restricting land ownership by foreigners. Huge amounts of money were at stake. Burr undertook to change the law, but asked for $5,000 to spread around among key legislators. Once the bill was passed, the Holland Company compensated Burr with a $5,000 loan he never had to pay back, and they also forgave another loan for $20,000.

There's a word for this sort of thing: bribery. John Barker Church threw that word around at a dinner, it got back to Burr, and he challenged Church to a duel. Church had probably learned about the shenanigans from Hamilton, who as a lawyer for the Holland Company was privy to what was going on. (In fact, the company had approached Hamilton first, but had balked when he demanded they pay to play by investing in his father-in-law's canal company. Of course, Hamilton was not a public official at the time.)

Alexander Hamilton had challenged perhaps half a dozen men to duels. Aaron Burr had never challenged anyone until now. It was not his style. As he wrote to a friend: "This, sir, is the first time in my life that I have condescended (pardon the expression) to refute calumny." Why now? Burr likely believed that Hamilton was the source of rumors going around about his role in the Holland deal, and saw an opportunity to send Hamilton a message. It is noteworthy that Burr chose for his second Aedanus Burke, the hotheaded South Carolina congressman who had almost fought a duel with Hamilton eight years earlier when Hamilton was treasury secretary.

Burr was remarkably cool when he arrived at the dueling ground in Weehawken for a sunset rendezvous. He chatted cheerfully with Church. They had a lot to talk about. Both were directors of the Manhattan Company, which had opened its doors the day before. Their easy conversation suggests Burr bore no personal grudge against Church, and was just trying to make a point.

At the appointed moment, both men fired simultaneously—and missed. Church's bullet came remarkably close to hitting Burr, piercing his coat. (One more moment when history could have taken a different turn.) As the seconds reloaded their guns for another shot, Church expressed regret for what he had said, calling his remarks "indiscreet." It was hardly a ringing apology, but Burr quickly accepted it, and everyone returned to New York. The next time Burr would cross the Hudson to fight a duel, he would meet Alexander Hamilton on the other side.

In December 1799, the man who would be called "first in war, first in peace, and first in the hearts of his countrymen" died at Mount Vernon. As the commander of the army that won the nation's independence, the president of the convention that brought forth the Constitution, and the chief executive who had held the country together during its formative years, George Washington was truly America's indispensable man. History has sculpted him in stone and cloaked him in august dignity. Behind the marble mask, however, was the intensely passionate leader who did so much to boost Hamilton's career and impede Burr's.

Fittingly, the last letter Washington wrote in his long public career was to the man who had served him in so many ways: Alexander Hamilton. It discussed Hamilton's efforts to create a military academy at West Point. "The establishment of an institution of this kind," wrote Washington, "has ever been considered by me as an object of primary importance to this country." (The idea would finally come to fruition under the presidency of Thomas Jefferson.) Hamilton mourned the passing of the man who had loomed so large in his life. "Perhaps no friend of his has more cause to lament on personal account than myself," he wrote. Death had robbed Hamilton of his most important ally.

Meantime, the war fever that had gripped the nation had cooled considerably. Public support for military preparations dwindled. Despite Hamilton's best efforts, the Provisional Army never amounted to more than two thousand men. Any thought that he might have a chance to lead the army into battle died when President Adams sent new envoys to France to negotiate a peace deal. Congress halted enlistments and by June 1800 the army was demobilized. It was a great personal disappointment to Hamilton that all his military efforts had been for naught.

The Federalists were in trouble. The Alien and Sedition Acts triggered an avalanche of opposition to President Adams, especially in the South. What's more, the president was at odds with other members of his own party. Back in 1775, John Adams had prodded reluctant delegates at the Continental Congress to declare American independence. Yet despite his obvious brilliance, his fiery temperament ill suited him for the presidency. He was prone to anger, stubborn, jealous, a man who nursed grudges and found it difficult to work with people. His cabinet members frequently turned to Hamilton for advice, and Hamilton was happy to offer it. Adams had become convinced that his cabinet was taking orders from Hamilton instead of him. In a fit of anger, he fired Secretary of War James McHenry and Secretary of State Timothy Pickering. Adams and Hamilton engaged in a personal showdown over the president's decision to pursue peace with France. Adams belittled Hamilton, whom he called the "Little Man," saying he was overwrought. "Never in my life did I hear a man talk more like a fool," Adams said with disdain. The party's two most prominent figures were at each other's throats.

It was becoming clear that the presidential election of 1800 would be a contest unrivaled in bitterness and fury. Once again, John Adams and Thomas Jefferson would be the opposing candidates. But if they were the big stars of what turned out to be the one of the most extraordinary election dramas in American history, Hamilton and Burr were the supporting actors who stole the show.

THREE

THE WILDEST ELECTION

Four years before

For New Yorkers, it was the juiciest murder trial in memory. First of all, it boasted a beautiful young victim, twenty-two-year-old Gulielma Sands, whose body was discovered at the bottom of a well three days before Christmas. Suspicious eyes quickly fell on her fiancé, a strapping young carpenter named Levi Weeks. Wagging tongues spread the lurid tale that Sands had been "generous with her favors" to Weeks, and that he had allegedly strangled her once she became pregnant. Weeks was arrested and accused. An outraged public condemned him from the outset. Sands's family further inflamed public opinion when they put her battered and bruised body on public display. The ghoulish spectacle captivated the entire city. "Scarcely anything else is spoken of," wrote one New Yorker.

The sensational trial began on March 31, 1800, and lasted three days. Enormous, rubbernecking crowds flocked to the courthouse. Those who managed to squeeze inside could hear people on the street chanting, "Crucify him, Crucify him!" Completing the "trial of the century" tableau (it was a new century, after all) was the all-star legal team assembled to defend the beleaguered defendant. It was led by New York's two most illustrious attorneys.

Alexander Hamilton and Aaron Burr.

Burr made the opening statement for the defense. A reporter covering the trial described it as "one of the most masterly speeches" he had ever heard. Fifty-five witnesses paraded before the jury. Burr and Hamilton worked together to demolish the prosecution witnesses and establish Weeks's alibi. After the final witness testified, it was up to Hamilton to give the closing statement. Confident of victory, he announced that since everyone was "sinking under fatigue" he would waive the summation. It was a rare example of Hamilton deciding that less was more. The jury deliberated for five minutes before declaring Weeks not guilty.

How did a young carpenter rate such a dazzling defense team? For one thing, his brother, Ezra Weeks, was a prominent builder who knew both Burr and Hamilton. He had already started work on The Grange, the new mansion Hamilton was building way out in the country—in Harlem. For another thing, the well where Sands was found turned out to belong to the Manhattan Company. Burr undoubtedly wanted to exercise some damage control. There was another more pressing motive for their involvement. The trial came just three weeks before local elections that would play a pivotal role in the presidential race. Both Burr and Hamilton had a reason to want the public spotlight shining on them. Neither could afford to leave the stage to the other. The trial of Levi Weeks was, in some ways, the opening act of the 1800 presidential election.

★ ★ ★

The election of 1800 was one of the most tumultuous in American history, a spectacle that made even the Weeks trial seem tame. Once again it would pit Jefferson against Adams, but the intensity of this conflict would be ratcheted up far higher than the election four years before. The contest was infused with such fury and desperation that it seemed to temporarily derange those involved. It ended in a photo finish never duplicated in American politics, changed the direction of the country, and left Hamilton's and Burr's reputations in tatters.

The Federalists had been in power for twelve years. Just eighteen months before, they had been riding a surge of popularity as they rallied the country for a threatened war against the French. Now, with the prospect of war all but gone, and a rising tide of hostility over the Alien and Sedition Acts, their support had cratered. They also suffered from being characterized as the party of the well-to-do or, as one Federalist smugly described his colleagues, "the wise, the rich and the well-born." Federalist leaders seemed to look down their noses at the hoi polloi, and expressed horror at the mob rule exemplified by the French Revolution. A sizable number of voters came to see the race as a battle between the poor and the rich, the common people and an inaccessible elite. All of this filled Republicans with optimism that this election could change the direction of America.

The stakes were high. For a dozen years the Federalists had controlled federal patronage. That gravy train would come to a screeching halt if they lost. They also feared that Thomas Jefferson would tear down the economic system that had been so carefully constructed by Alexander Hamilton, thus ruining the nation's trade and commerce. Deep down they worried about something worse. They feared that Jefferson would lead an upheaval akin to the French Revolution and tear the country to shreds.

The Republicans believed that if Adams prevailed, it would lead to unbridled tyranny. The Federalists might leverage the win to cement permanent political power and use the Alien and Sedition Acts to jail anyone who opposed them. Furthermore, Republicans were disturbed at the growth in deficit spending and taxes. They believed that only a Jefferson victory could secure the individual rights that Americans had fought for in their own revolution.

The fervent belief that so much was at stake—indeed, that the fate of the new nation might be in peril—fueled unparalleled personal attacks and stirred deep-seated paranoia. President Adams was decried as warmonger, a tyrant, a criminal. Republican editor James Callender mocked him as a "poor old man" and a "hideous, hermaphroditical character." Jefferson was labeled an atheist, and apocalyptic prophecies were made about a Jefferson presidency. "Murder, robbery, rape, adultery, and incest will all be openly taught and practiced," predicted the *Connecticut Courant*. "The air will be rent with the cries of distress, the soil will be soaked with blood, and the nation black with crimes." Reverend Thomas Dwight, president of Yale, blustered that under a Jefferson presidency "we may see the Bible cast into the bonfire . . . we may see our wives and daughters the victims of legal prostitution." Housewives in New England buried their Bibles in the gardens, convinced that, as president, Jefferson would confiscate and burn them.

The outlines of the election were clear. New England was expected to go for Adams. Pennsylvania would split. The South would be solidly for Jefferson. The pivotal state was likely to be New York, with twelve electoral votes, more than any other state except Virginia, with twenty-one. New York's presidential electors were appointed by the state's General Assembly. Therefore, the most crucial election would be the one held in April to elect state representatives. With the upstate vote largely balanced between Federalists and Republicans, it would all come down to the election for state representatives from the New York City area. If Republicans could win those seats, a perfect political cascade would ensue: they could control the legislature and the state's electoral vote, and they would have the ability to steer the national election in their favor.

Aaron Burr believed he was the man who could pull off this feat. If he succeeded, it would catapult his political career forward. It might even move him within reach of juicy political plums such as governor, vice president, or perhaps someday even president. To make that happen, he would have to best Alexander Hamilton.

Burr might have lost his legislative seat in 1799, but he continued to build his organization in the state and forge stronger contacts with Republicans elsewhere. He was seen nationally as a bold and intrepid political leader. The *Philadelphia Aurora* praised Burr's "ardent devotion to the principles of liberty," while admiring his energetic decisiveness. "While other men are debating, he resolves, and while they resolve, he acts." Now he was ready to act decisively to seize control of the election. He made a quick trip to Philadelphia in 1800 to confer with Thomas Jefferson. Then he got down to work, depending as always on the small team of New York political allies known as the Burrites.

Burr waited for Hamilton and the Federalists to draw up their ticket of candidates, which largely consisted of unknowns, including a baker, a potter, a shoemaker, and two grocers. The Federalists may have been trying to counter their elitist image, or perhaps those were simply the best candidates they could find. In any case, Burr responded with a masterstroke: a dream team of candidates that included former governor George Clinton, General Horatio Gates, who had won the Battle of Saratoga, and other popular Republican leaders. It had taken all of his charm and persuasiveness to convince these heavy hitters to run in an election for state legislature, but it gave his ticket a luster the Federalists could not match.

While Hamilton was one of the country's most innovative statesmen, Burr stood out as a groundbreaking pioneer in the art of politics. For years he had honed his tradecraft. Now, he unleashed a dazzling array of innovative practices designed to defeat the Federalists. He held regular political meetings at Martling's Tavern, which also happened to be the headquarters for a new and politically active club known as Tammany Society. (Eventually, it would grow into New York's legendary political powerhouse, Tammany Hall.) Burr created a political organization run by a central committee with tentacles reaching down to the ward level. In the weeks before the election, he threw open the doors to his own house to campaign workers, offering them meals and sleeping accommodations.

To marshal support for his ticket, Burr drew on his experiences in the Revolution, when he was keeping the peace in war-ravaged Westchester County. Back then he put together a register of names that categorized people's allegiance, and the degree of their fervor. Now he prepared a roster of every voter in the city. Campaign workers went door to door to note each voter's political preferences, the depth of his commitment (only men could vote at that time), his financial standing, and his willingness to volunteer. Burr used this to guide both fund-raising and voter turnout efforts.

In an era when most candidates didn't deign to campaign for themselves, Burr unhesitatingly took to the streets to press the flesh.

A Federalist newspaper, *The Daily Advertiser,* wondered how a "would-be vice president could stoop so low as to visit every corner in search of voters." All these techniques seem commonplace today. They were virtually unheard of before Burr put them into practice.

Hamilton was distracted by his duties as the acting commander of the Provisional Army, which had not yet been disbanded. Nevertheless, he, too, became personally involved in campaigning for the Federalist ticket during the legislative elections. A Republican newspaper noted that "Every day he is seen in the street hurrying this way, and darting that; here he buttons a heavy hearted Fed and preaches up courage, there he meets a group and he simpers in unanimity." Like Burr, he set an exhaustive pace. "Never have I witnessed such exertions on either side before," said his friend Robert Troup, worn out from trying to keep up with Hamilton. "I have not eaten dinner for three days and have been constantly upon my legs from 7 in the morning 'til 7 in the afternoon."

Voting took place over three days from April 29 to May 1. Burr made arrangements for carriages and wagons to bring Republican voters to the polls. He sent German-speaking canvassers into the German wards to urge voters there to turn out. He dispatched volunteers to polling places to guard against trickery or errors. He himself spent ten hours at one polling place where he was particularly concerned about election fraud.

The Republicans triumphed. They swept the voting in greater New York City, winning all the legislative seats from that area, which shifted the balance of power in the General Assembly from the Federalists to the Republicans. Burr was downright gleeful. "We have beaten you with superior management!" he gloated to one Federalist.

Hamilton, knowing full well what the election meant, was utterly distraught. "A new and a more dangerous era has commenced," he mourned. "Revolution and a new order of things are avowed in this corner. Property, liberty and even life are at stake."

The absolute victory engineered by his rival evidently left Hamilton unhinged. Washington, his mentor and patron, had died just months before. His army was being dismantled. His influence was on the wane. Now the barbarians were at the gate; indeed, they had broken through. Hamilton worked himself into a state of hyperanxiety that would lead to a series of bizarre outbursts and actions as the year went on.

His immediate response was to try to change the rules of the game. He implored New York governor John Jay to convene a special legislative session, before the Republican legislators took office, in order to change the way presidential electors were selected. Hamilton called for direct election by congressional district, which would deny the Republicans some of New York's electoral vote. Hamilton understood that this was a partisan move that smacked of extreme political chicanery. That was not enough of a reason to hold back, he told Jay. "It will not do to be overscrupulous...by a strict adherence to ordinary rules." Jefferson, he declared breathlessly, "was an *Atheist* in Religion and a *Fanatic* in politics," and thus extraordinary measures were justified to bar him from office. Jay, more coolheaded than Hamilton, understood that such a move would tear the state apart. He ignored Hamilton's note.

The national election would be run the same way as the election four years earlier. Electors would each cast two votes. At least one of the two votes had to be for an out-of-state candidate. The parties might specify who was running for president, and who for vice president, but that didn't affect the way the votes were tallied. Once again, it was a four-way race. The top vote getter among the four candidates would become president, and the runner-up would serve as vice president.

Burr was the man of the hour, and the obvious Republican pick to run for vice president alongside Thomas Jefferson. "His generalship, perseverance, industry and execution exceeds all description," exclaimed a prominent New York Republican named James Nicholson. "He deserves anything and everything of his country." Burr, flush with electoral success and considering a campaign for governor, was reluctant to accept. When the subject was broached, one witness said he shouted "that he would not give up the certainty of being elected governor to the uncertainty of being chosen vice president." Burr well remembered how southern electors, especially those from Virginia, had abandoned him in the last election, casting their first vote for Jefferson, then throwing away their second vote instead of giving it to him. If he ran with Jefferson, he wanted assurances that he wouldn't be played the fool again.

He got them. When Republican congressmen unanimously nominated Burr for vice president on May 11, 1800, they also passed a resolution directing *all* Republican electors to vote for both the party's presidential and vice-presidential candidates. No one, they said, should throw away a vote. This push to enforce party unity would circle back to haunt them.

Once he agreed to run, Burr, true to form, threw himself into the race. He made an extended campaign trip to New England to see if he could pry some votes away from Adams. He also set up a network of supporters to press his case in other states. He wanted to demonstrate to southern electors that he was a force to be reckoned with. "I was really averse to have my name in question," he wrote to a friend, "but being so, it is most obvious I should not choose to be trifled with."

Hamilton must have been beside himself. Three out of four candidates in the campaign were people he considered enemies. The only one he really respected was the Federalist candidate for vice president, Charles Cotesworth Pinckney, who had become famous for standing up to the French in the XYZ Affair. (He also happened to be the brother of Adams's 1796 running mate—the only time that happened in U.S. history.) Even with New York in Jefferson's column, the election would be close. Publicly, Hamilton told people that supporting Adams and Pinckney equally was "the only thing that can possibly save us from the fangs of *Jefferson.*" Privately he cooked up a desperate scheme to engineer a long-shot victory for Pinckney. It proved to be one of the most disastrous moves of his career.

Hamilton wrote a fifty-page pamphlet arguing that Adams was temperamentally unfit to be president (a charge that is still trumpeted in presidential campaigns two hundred years later). He apparently planned to print a small number of copies and distribute them sub rosa to electors in South Carolina, Pinckney's home state, right before they voted in December. Hamilton hoped that some electors would vote for Pinckney but not Adams, thus ensuring that if the Federalists won, Pinckney would be elected president.

Hamilton held nothing back. He berated the president's "disgusting egotism" and deplored his "ungovernable temper," asserting that, "he is often liable to paroxysms of anger which deprive him of self-command and produce very outrageous behavior." That sentence—describing Adams—succinctly depicted Hamilton himself.

How could a man of his intelligence and experience conceive that a lengthy diatribe directed at a sitting president—his own party's candidate—was a prudent tactic? It clearly was not a product of cool political acumen, but a display of anger, jealousy, and resentment. Hamilton seemed to be careening off the rails.

Then, as now, it was nearly impossible to keep something that juicy under wraps. Hamilton's plan went horribly awry when a copy of his pamphlet fell into the hands of his enemies, who rushed it into print in October. Republicans were ecstatic. James Madison described it as a "thunderbolt" that could only help ensure his party's victory. "I rejoice with you," he wrote Jefferson, "that Republicanism is likely to be *completely* triumphant."

Hamilton's invective-laden essay on Adams (formally titled "Letter from Alexander Hamilton, Concerning the Public Conduct and Character of John Adams, Esq., President of the United States") proved to be a devastating self-inflicted injury.

Federalists were appalled that Hamilton had attacked their standard bearer in the throes of a close election. Federalist editor Noah Webster called it "little short of insanity." Even his friend Robert Troup agreed that it showed "his character is radically deficient in discretion... Hence he is considered as an unfit head of the party." Adams's public response was remarkably restrained, but privately he raged. Years later he revealed the depths of his own bitterness when he blamed Hamilton's strange behavior on "a superabundance of excretions which he [Hamilton] could not find whores enough to draw off."

In the midst of the tumultuous presidential race, another momentous event took place. The federal government moved from Philadelphia to Washington. The new capital was still just a sleepy village dotted with unfinished government buildings and construction shacks. Nearby swamps bred abundant clouds of mosquitos, and many of the town's unpaved roads still had tree stumps in them. On November 1, 1800, John and Abigail Adams moved into the drafty White House that slaves and paid laborers were still working on. Congress convened later that month in the small section of the Capitol building that had been hastily completed.

The day most Americans considered "election day" was December 3, when electors gathered in their respective state capitals to vote. By mid-December, it was clear the Republicans had triumphed. "Mr. Jefferson may, therefore, be considered our future president," proclaimed the *National Intelligencer* newspaper. Adams said he had been defeated in "a squall of thunder and lightning and hail, attended by a strong smell of sulfur," not so subtly suggesting that with Jefferson in charge, Satan held the reins.

Jefferson, however, was not in charge yet. There was a wrinkle. Since the Constitution didn't differentiate between votes for president or vice president, Jefferson and Burr had tied. Each had seventy-three electoral votes. The calls for party unity had proven more successful than people imagined. Not a single elector had withheld a vote for Burr. Under the Constitution, this meant that the House of Representatives would decide the outcome of the presidential race. Hamilton and the Federalists still had a chance to keep Jefferson out of the brand-new White House. "This has produced great dismay & gloom on the Republican gentlemen here," wrote Jefferson, "and equal exultation in the Federalists, who openly declare they will prevent an election."[5]

5. The quirk in the Constitution that led to this brouhaha was changed in 1803 with passage of the Twelfth Amendment, which directed electors to cast separate votes for president and vice president.

The Federalists would need to act swiftly—they had just two months plus a few days. Electoral votes would not be officially announced until February 11, 1801. On that day the House would be compelled to vote on whether Jefferson or Burr would be president. Each state would have one vote. Nine votes would win it. The Republicans controlled only eight of the sixteen state delegations, not enough to secure a Jefferson victory. The Federalists controlled six. The remaining two states were split. For the next two months, plotting and scheming would be the order of the day. Most of it would center on Aaron Burr.

Federalists in Congress who were eager to block Jefferson proposed various schemes. Eventually, they determined that supporting Burr was their best option. Since Burr had not committed himself to the "pernicious principles" of Jefferson, they considered him a man they could at least deal with. Many regarded him as the lesser of two evils. They reckoned Burr would be more receptive to a strong national government than Jefferson, and less likely to dismantle the financial structure erected by Hamilton. Stung by the divisions in their own party, they also hoped to sow similar discord among their opponents. If Burr won the presidency with Federalist help, he would be considered a backstabber by fellow Republicans, and would be obliged to align with Federalists to get things done.

Burr could have undermined the Federalist maneuvers simply by declaring that he would not accept the presidency. At first, that's what it seemed he was going to do. As the election results began to come in, Burr wrote to Congressman Samuel Smith of Maryland, a friend who was also a close Jefferson ally, suggesting that in the case of a tie, he would happily yield to Jefferson: "Every man who knows me, ought to know that I should utterly disclaim all competition." A few days later he wrote directly to Jefferson, saying he would support him no matter what happened. "My personal friends are perfectly informed of my wishes on the subject and can never think of diverting a single vote from you...I see no reason to doubt of you having at least nine states if the business shall come before the House of Representatives."

Once all the votes were in and it was certain that Jefferson and Burr had tied, however, Burr's tone changed dramatically. He made it crystal clear in a second letter to Smith that if the House of Representatives chose him as president he would NOT resign. He reiterated this when he met with Smith the first week in January in Philadelphia, adding that if he *was* elected, all Republicans should support him.

Smith reported all this back to Jefferson. Soon word leaked out that Burr was angling for the presidency after all. "By persons friendly to Mr. Burr, it is distinctly stated that he is willing to consider the Federalists as his friends & to accept the office of President as their gift," wrote Federalist James Bayard, Delaware's sole member of Congress. Thomas Jefferson was convinced of the same thing, even suspecting that Burr was spreading around bribes to secure support. "Burr...has agents here at work," he wrote.

Burr, true to form, was pursuing a wait-and-see gambit. He was not ready to fully declare himself. He would accept if the presidency was offered, but he would not overtly seek the office. He would let the game come to him. It is easy to ascribe his decision to ambition, which certainly played a role. A schemer driven solely by ambition, however, would likely have made a more aggressive grab for the brass ring. Burr may also have been motivated by the belief that the party and country would be better served by him accepting the presidency than by the Federalists somehow usurping the election. In any case, he bided his time.

Back in New York City, Hamilton observed the unfolding drama. One of his guiding principles over the last few years had been to keep Jefferson from becoming president. Jefferson, after all, was the great Satan who might destroy the country. How many words had Hamilton poured out to that purpose? "All personal and partial considerations must be discarded," he had argued four years earlier, "and everything must give way to the great object of excluding Jefferson." Here was an opportunity to bar the door of the White House to the hated Republican who had so tormented him, and Hamilton might have been expected to embrace the plan concocted by his fellow Federalists.

He did just the opposite. "There is no doubt," he wrote to Treasury Secretary Oliver Wolcott Jr. in December, "that upon every virtuous and prudent calculation Jefferson is to be preferred. He is by far not so dangerous a man." This was an astonishing assertion from Hamilton. Jefferson was less dangerous than Burr? Hamilton was expressing a point of view diametrically opposed to what almost every other Federalist believed. It was only his first salvo.

Hamilton unleashed a blizzard of letters to Federalists in Washington, attacking Burr and pleading with them to support Jefferson. Once again Hamilton left no stone unturned, rising to new heights of vehemence. His language verged on the hysterical.

"This man has no principle public or private."

"Burr loves nothing but himself; thinks of nothing but his own aggrandizement, and will be content with nothing short of permanent power in his own hands."

"He is in every sense a profligate; a voluptuary in the extreme."

"He is bankrupt beyond redemption except by the plunder of his country."

"The haughtiest of men, he is at the same time the most creeping to answer his purposes."

"I could scarcely name a discreet man of either party in our State, who does not think Mr. Burr the most unfit man in the U.S. for the office of President. Disgrace abroad [and] ruin at home are the probable fruits of his elevation."

"For Heaven's sake my dear Sir, exert yourself to the utmost to save our country from so great a calamity."

The idea that Burr might become president made Hamilton apoplectic. Did Hamilton believe Burr was a threat to the nation, to the Federalist party, or to his own political future? Possibly all three. Hamilton certainly knew Burr as well as anyone in the Federalist party, and may well have had serious doubts about his fitness for office. Yet the torrent of words and the shrill tone suggested a visceral hatred that went beyond politics. Burr had displaced Jefferson as Hamilton's most hated enemy. Jefferson, he argued, had "pretentions to character." Burr had none. Burr had made it personal when he betrayed Hamilton in the Holland Company deal, challenged John Church to a duel, and outmaneuvered Hamilton in the New York elections. It appeared that all of Hamilton's resentments over his own fall from grace were now aimed squarely at his cool and calculating New York rival, who was poised to outstrip him.

Certain Federalists contemplated making a deal with Burr in exchange for their support. Treasury Secretary Oliver Wolcott, Jr. broached this in a letter to Hamilton: "Can any terms be obtained from Mr. Burr favorable to the true interest of the country, and is he a man who will adhere to terms when stipulated?" Hamilton scoffed at such an idea: "No engagement that can be made with him can be depended upon. While making it he will laugh in his sleeve at the credulity of those with whom he makes it—and the first moment it suits his views to break it he will do so." Instead, Hamilton urged his fellow Federalists to make a deal with Jefferson, and agree to support the Virginian only if he agreed not to meddle with the financial system, not to thwart efforts to enlarge the navy, and to remain neutral in the conflict between France and England.

Hamilton's arguments had little effect on most of the Federalists in Congress. His judgment was in question and his influence on the decline, especially after the Adams brouhaha. Besides which, most Federalists hated Jefferson above all other Republicans. Hamilton's words did make an impression, however, on James Bayard, the congressman from Delaware. A heavyset man, described as poised and impressive, Bayard was Delaware's sole member of Congress. His single vote would be pivotal. Hamilton directed several letters to Bayard, expressing his "extreme alarm" that Federalists were supporting Burr. He went so far as to say that if Burr was elected with Federalist support, he would consider himself "an isolated man" and would leave the party that "degraded itself & the Country." Bayard was torn about what to do. He shared some of Hamilton's concerns, but worried that the government "would not survive the course of moral & political experiments to which it would be subjected in the hands of Mr. Jefferson." He eventually decided to join his fellow Federalists in backing Burr, and see what course events would take.

As the day of reckoning drew closer, tensions in Washington escalated. Every dawn gave rise to new rumors. There were murmurings of an assassination plot against Jefferson, of Federalists stockpiling arms, of Virginians preparing to march on the capital. The Republican governor of Pennsylvania let it be known that if the Federalists tried to steal the election he would call out the militia. Jefferson took the talk of political shenanigans seriously enough that he visited the White House to issue President Adams a warning. A Federalist attempt "to defeat the Presidential election" would "produce resistance by force, and incalculable results."

Congressman Bayard wrote a family member to say it was "certainly within the compass of possibility that Burr may ultimately obtain nine [states]." He kept Hamilton updated on the situation. "I take it for granted that Mr. B would not only gladly accept the office, but will neglect no means in his power to secure it." For someone who was allegedly scheming to be president, though, Burr displayed a remarkably blasé attitude. As the days counted down to the House vote, he was consumed by another event: the wedding of his darling daughter Theodosia to Joseph Alston, a wealthy young man from South Carolina. The marriage took place on Monday, February 2, just nine days before the critical tiebreaker vote in the House. The day after the wedding, Burr headed back to Albany, where the New York state legislature was going into session.

During all this time, Burr preserved a careful silence about what was going on in Washington. He certainly must have heard about Hamilton's overwrought attacks. Still, he wrote no letters defending his character, no letters pleading for support or clarifying his position. Federalist Robert Goodloe Harper, congressman from South Carolina, assured him this was the best strategy: "Keep the game perfectly in your hands," he wrote, "but do not answer this letter or any other." Burr watched and waited. By early February, Jefferson was convinced that Burr must be cooperating and coordinating with Federalists, but there was no tangible evidence to prove that.

A storm blanketed Washington, D.C., with snow on the morning of Wednesday, February 11, and members of the House had to trudge uphill through snowdrifts to reach the Capitol. One congressman went through truly herculean efforts to attend. Republican Joseph Hopper Nicholson from Maryland was battling pneumonia and found himself gripped by a raging fever. With his state's delegation deadlocked, he needed to show up to prevent the Federalists from giving Burr Maryland's vote. So Nicholson ordered bearers to carry him in on a stretcher from his home two miles away. "There is a chance this kills him," wrote Massachusetts congressman Harrison Gray Otis. "I would not thus expose myself for any president on earth." Nicholson proceeded to do the same thing every day that the House deliberated the election. Each time there was a ballot, his wife brought it to him as he lay in the antechamber so he could cast his vote. Nicholson survived the ordeal. A dozen years later he was instrumental in publishing a poem by his brother-in-law, Francis Scott Key, titled "The Defense of Fort McHenry." Or, as we know it today, "The Star Spangled Banner."

Their first order of business on Wednesday, February 11, was to officially count the electoral votes. The House and Senate convened together for this task, presided over by the man most affected by the outcome: Thomas Jefferson. There were no surprises. Jefferson and Burr were tied at seventy-three votes apiece. The House then convened separately to vote on which of the two men would become president of the United States.

The first ballot showed eight states for Jefferson, six for Burr, and two tied. After fourteen more ballots, nothing had changed. They adjourned for dinner and returned for four more ballots in the dimly lit chamber. By 3:30 A.M., when they took their last vote, many congressmen were dropping with fatigue. "The contest would seem to be who has the most strength of constitution, or who is most able to bear fatigue," wrote the New York *Commercial Advertiser.* They adjourned for the night.

Balloting continued on Thursday, Friday, and Saturday. No change. Frustrations were growing, and the members of the House were operating under a deadline. The Constitution required that the inauguration be held on March 4. Should the election not be decided by then, the capital, and indeed the entire nation, would be in an uproar.

Sunday, the fifteenth, was supposed to be a day of rest, but no. Instead, it was a day of whispered conferences and furtive negotiations. Fresh reports came in, indicating that Republicans were preparing to take up arms. The *Washington Federalist* claimed that "ten thousand Republican swords will leap from their scabbards" if Jefferson wasn't elected. Two Federalists announced they had received death threats.

Delaware's James Bayard wondered if the country was going to come apart. Republicans, it seemed, would "rather see the union dissolved...than give up Jefferson." He decided that the time had come to heed Hamilton's advice and make the best deal with Jefferson that he could. Working through Congressman Samuel Smith, Jefferson's ally, Bayard received assurances that Jefferson would not tamper with Hamilton's financial system, reduce the size of the navy, or take France's side against England. In a Federalist caucus on Monday, Bayard announced that he would throw Delaware to Jefferson. Some of his fellow Federalists labeled him a deserter, but his decision broke the deadlock. In the end, Bayard didn't have to change his vote. His stated intention to vote for Jefferson, if he had to, convinced some of his Federalist colleagues to abstain from voting. That threw Maryland and Vermont to Jefferson, and on the thirty-sixth ballot he was at last declared the new president.

Jefferson always denied that he made the deal that Bayard outlined, though evidence suggests that he did, feeling it was his only clear route to the presidency. Congressman Smith denied that there was a deal until he was forced to testify about it under oath at a trial years later—when he suddenly made an about-face and admitted that he had, in fact, brokered such a deal. The best proof may be that Jefferson, as president, closely adhered to the terms that Hamilton had suggested and Bayard had proposed.

The Federalists apparently offered Burr a similar deal if he wanted their continued support. After the third day of balloting, Federalist congressman William Cooper declared, "Had Burr done anything for himself he would long ere this have been president." Bayard later informed Hamilton that "means existed of electing Burr, but this required his co-operation." Burr apparently considered making a last-minute trip from Albany to Washington, and even packed his bags in anticipation of the trip, but then decided against it. Had Burr played ball with Federalists looking for a deal, they might have held out longer; some Republicans might have come over to his side to avert a crisis; he might have become president.

Burr's modus operandi of playing things close to the vest, and being unwilling to commit himself, hurt him badly. "Burr has acted a miserable paltry part," Bayard wrote. He was too proud to renounce his aspirations, too cautious to exploit the situation. True, he had achieved the office of vice president, but he was serving a president and a party who no longer trusted him. He had also alienated Federalists by remaining on the fence. He was a man apart.

March 4, 1801, was the day of Jefferson's inauguration. George Washington and John Adams had ridden to their ceremonies in elegant carriages, decked out in their finest clothes (Washington donned a uniform), wearing powdered wigs and carrying military swords. Jefferson wanted to send a message that a Republican administration would be different. He wore a simple suit with no wig or sword, and he walked the unpaved roads from the boardinghouse where he had been living since early December to the Capitol. There he shook hands perfunctorily with Vice President Aaron Burr, who introduced him to the assembled crowd of about a thousand people. Jefferson sounded a conciliatory tone in his Inaugural Address. "We are all republicans, we are all federalists," he said. (His text left the words uncapitalized—he was referring to philosophy, not the actual parties.)

Nevertheless, both Burr and Hamilton found themselves estranged from their respective parties. The election of 1800 had left them bruised and battered, wielding little or no power. Each was looking for a way to put his life back on track, and each had reason to blame the other for their political derailment. It wouldn't be long before their simmering grudge match escalated into a final confrontation.

★ ★ ★ ★ ★ TWO ★ ★ ★ ★ ★

THE FINAL COUNTDOWN

Three years before

The two antagonists rowed across the Hudson River to the New Jersey shore. There they would settle their differences on the dueling ground. Their seconds loaded the ornate dueling pistols owned by John Barker Church and paced off the distance between the two men. According to long-established custom, the duelists stood sideways, presenting the narrowest possible profile to their opponent. Once the duel commenced, Hamilton held his fire, as if daring his opponent to shoot first. Nearly a minute passed before Hamilton's foe raised his pistol and fired. The shot ripped into Hamilton just above his hip and went all the way through. Hamilton fired his pistol wide and wild before he crashed to the ground. He was rowed back across the Hudson, where he died in agony the next day.

But it was not Alexander Hamilton who was killed this day, November 23, 1801. It was his twenty-year-old son Philip, fighting a duel that would eerily foreshadow the Hamilton-Burr encounter three years later. Even before his son's death, Hamilton had felt his fortunes fading. Now he would plunge deeper into despair than he could ever imagine.

Jefferson's inauguration ten months earlier, in March 1801, cast Hamilton into political exile. No longer was he at the center of national events with a pipeline into the cabinet. The people running the country were not interested in his advice. Even many of his fellow Federalists now questioned his judgment. It was a dizzying demise. When he campaigned on behalf of the Federalist candidate for governor of New York, people denounced him as a thief, a rascal, and a villain. Hamilton felt forgotten and scorned. "What can I do better than withdraw from the scene?" he wrote bitterly. "Every day proves to me more and more that this American world was not made for me."

Hamilton focused much of his energy on completing The Grange, the mansion he was building on a thirty-two-acre estate, ten miles north of New York City. Named after the ancestral home in Scotland that his father had left so long ago, it was situated in the rolling hills of Harlem Heights, near today's 143rd Street. Hamilton hired John McComb Jr., the architect for Gracie Mansion, to design a two-story frame house big enough for his large family. Completed in the summer of 1802, the Federal-style home featured large verandas on either side that commanded views of both the Harlem and the Hudson Rivers flowing down either side of Manhattan. The entryway was graced by a Gilbert Stuart portrait of George Washington that Washington himself had presented to Hamilton as a gift.

Here Hamilton could distance himself from the political storms that had left him marooned. He spent more time with his family. He walked the grounds of his country estate, trying to find the peace that had eluded him. "A disappointed politician is very apt to take refuge in a garden," he joked to a friend. The house and land put him deeply in debt, but he was sure that in time his law practice would enable him to pay it back. He remained a lightning rod for controversy. It was, in fact, an attack on Hamilton that provoked his eldest son's duel.

New York Republicans planned a big celebration for July 4, 1801. After all, their recently elected president had written the Declaration of Independence. A twenty-seven-year-old Republican attorney named George Eacker spoke at the festivities. Eacker was known for his oratorical skills and used them to heap abuse on Alexander Hamilton. He charged that Hamilton had raised the Provisional Army not to fight the French, but to intimidate Republicans under "pretended apprehension of a foreign invasion." Hamilton had grown thick-skinned enough to brush off such charges, but the speech made his son's blood boil.

At nineteen, Philip Hamilton was smart and handsome. "Philip inherits his father's talents," Angelica Church told her sister. He had impressed his professors at Columbia College, where he had followed in his father's footsteps. Hamilton regarded him as the family's "brightest hope," and had high expectations for his firstborn child. Like his father, however, Philip was impetuous and a bit of a hell-raiser. Those qualities would undo him.

Philip Hamilton spotted Eacker at a Broadway show one Friday night in November. He and his friend Richard Price broke into Eacker's box and taunted him. "It is too abominable to be insulted by a set of rascals," Eacker snarled. "Rascal" was a trigger word almost guaranteed to result in a challenge to a duel. Price fought a hastily arranged duel with Eacker that Sunday. They went through several rounds of firing at each other, but neither party was injured. The two men declared that honor had been served. Eacker seemed not to take Price's participation very seriously—it was Hamilton who he thought had really insulted him. They agreed to duel the next day, a Monday.

Hamilton agonized over what to tell his son. Ultimately, he advised Philip to wait for Eacker to fire first, then to throw away his own shot. This, he felt, was the morally superior way of handling the situation. Philip could defend his father's honor and demonstrate his courage without making himself a murderer. Of course, this strategy depended on his opponent missing or choosing not to fire. Eacker did neither.

Gravely wounded, Philip was rowed back across the Hudson and brought to the nearby home of John Barker Church. Hamilton summoned his doctor, David Hosack. The anguished father actually fainted at Hosack's house and had to be revived before he could hurry to his son's side. When he saw Philip, he turned to Hosack, clutched his hands, and said quietly, "Doctor, I despair." Eliza also rushed to Philip's bedside, frantic with fear for her son's life.

Philip lived in agony for fourteen hours after he was shot, dying before dawn. Hamilton was crushed by his own heartache, and worried that Eliza, three months pregnant with their eighth child, might miscarry. While she eventually gave birth to another son, whom they also named Philip, there was another family casualty. Deranged by the death of her older brother, Philip's seventeen-year-old sister Angelica suffered a mental breakdown from which she never recovered.

The tragedies that befell his children tore at Hamilton. "Never did I see a man so completely overwhelmed with grief," said his friend

Robert Troup. Hamilton temporarily withdrew from politics—until Aaron Burr unintentionally dragged him back in.

In Washington, Burr found himself the odd man out in the Jefferson administration. The new president was convinced that Burr had connived against him in the election, and he was cool to the vice president, to say the least. Jefferson failed to consult him on cabinet selections. He flatly refused to appoint Burr's friend and trusted lieutenant Matthew Livingston Davis to a coveted post, despite Treasury Secretary Albert Gallatin's sharp warning that Burr would regard that rejection as a slap in the face. Burr felt isolated from the rest of the executive branch. He even joked to his daughter about how disconnected he was. "I...now and then meet the [cabinet] ministers in the street."

He strove to preside over the Senate with an even hand. Federalist congressman William Plumer of New Hampshire praised Burr for the way he undertook his duties "with great ease and dignity." Plumer said Burr "despises the littleness and meanness of the administration but does not distinctly oppose them or aid us." This approach won him no friends among the Republicans, while many Federalists remained distrustful.

Burr could see that he would never succeed in Jefferson's Republican party. So the man who was never too firmly attached to any political ideology made overtures to the Federalists. In February 1802, he created quite a commotion when he showed up at a Federalist gathering in Washington to celebrate the birthday of his old antagonist George Washington. Burr raised eyebrows further with his toast: "To a union of all honest men." Everyone knew this signaled a break with Jefferson and a move to ally himself more closely with the opposition party.

Alexander Hamilton, still grief-stricken over the loss of his son, was appalled. "Is it possible that some new intrigue is about to link the Federalists with a man who can never be anything else other than the bane of a good cause?"

The Federalists were deeply divided. Their party was almost in ruins. Its two most forceful leaders, Adams and Hamilton, had been shunted off to the sidelines. The "Virginia Junta," as they referred to Jefferson and Madison, was riding high. Prospects for the Federalist party were dim. Hamilton worried that "an eagerness to recover lost power" made the Federalists vulnerable to Burr's blandishments. He also fretted that if Burr became the Federalist darling, Hamilton's own place in the party would sink even further. It was a punch in the gut. He reacted accordingly, telling friends that it would be "disgraceful and ruinous" to cozy up to Burr, and would result in "political suicide." He stood ready to fight the usurper every inch of the way.

This was politics turned upside down. Burr, the sitting Republican vice president, was angling to restart his career with the support of the Federalists. Members of Burr's own party now became his bitter opponents. The political crossfire was especially chaotic in New York, where Burr soon found himself under ferocious attack from publications supported by New York Republicans. A slew of pamphlets, broadsides (posters), and newspaper articles painted him in the darkest of hues, in what became known as the "Pamphlet Wars of 1802–1804."

This battle took place amid a "wild west" media landscape that was a precursor to that of the twenty-first century. New publications kept popping up, each tilting toward a different political candidate, and most focused more on character assassination than reporting. Three recently launched New York papers were at the center of the political fray.

The *American Citizen,* supported by mainstream New York Republicans, launched many of the most damaging attacks on Burr. Editor James Cheetham was Thomas Jefferson's newest attack dog— he kept Jefferson informed about what he was up to, and Jefferson cheered him on from a distance. Aaron Burr and his supporters responded to the attacks by starting their own paper, the *Morning Chronicle*. They chose as editor an erudite young man named Peter Irving, whose then nineteen-year-old brother Washington Irving would go on to great literary fame. *The New York Evening Post* was founded by Alexander Hamilton in the hopes of reviving his and his party's fortunes.

Hamilton's paper was the only one of the three that survived—it thrives today as the *New York Post*. Its first editor was a Massachusetts lawyer and journalist named William Coleman, who came to be known as the "Field Marshal of Federal Editors." In this particular fight, however, Coleman took Burr's part. He had briefly been Burr's law partner, and even though his newspaper leaned Federalist, Coleman declared to potential investors that "in each party are honest and virtuous men." He apparently considered Burr to be an honest man, even if Hamilton did not.

The personal attacks were savage. No punch was too low. One broadside accused Burr of having debauched "numerous unhappy wretches" and consorted with courtesans of every description. Salvos of pamphlets and articles charged Burr with having run for vice president with the sole purpose of trying to usurp Jefferson. "The moment he was nominated, he put into operation a most extensive, complicated, and wicked scheme of intrigue to place himself in the presidential chair...he seems to have carried on a *secret* correspondence with the Federalists." Burr's allies shot back. New York attorney William Van Ness wrote passionate pamphlets in Burr's defense. The *Morning Chronicle* printed Burr's explicit denial that he had tried to make a deal with the Federalists to bring down Jefferson.

Charge and countercharge escalated tempers to a high pitch and duels ensued.

A Burr protégé, unhappy with attacks from the *American Citizen,* drew pistols with DeWitt Clinton, the governor's nephew, who was one of the primary backers of that paper. No one was hurt. Editor William Coleman faced off against a Jefferson supporter who took umbrage at his defense of Burr. He fatally shot the man before calmly returning to his newspaper office to get out the next edition.

Burr found himself under attack from Federalist and Republican alike. At first he was able to shrug off the onslaughts, just as he always had. He understood that politics was a rough-and-tumble business. Eventually, though, he began to seethe. He himself had never resorted to the rabid personal attacks that were aimed at him now, and he found them galling. Cheetham was especially vicious in his *American Citizen.* He used Hamilton to bait Burr, questioning in print why Burr had not challenged Hamilton to a duel over his vicious abuse of Burr's character. Cheetham wondered if Burr was "so degraded as to permit even General Hamilton to slander him with impunity." This provocative stick in the eye came in January 1804, six months before the showdown at Weehawken.

That was about the same time Burr made his move. Longtime New York Republican leader George Clinton, elected governor for a three-year term in 1801, had tired of the job and chose not to run for reelection in 1804. President Jefferson, distrusting Burr and determined to drop him from the ticket, picked Clinton as his running mate. (Presumably, that job would not be as fatiguing as running New York State!) Burr, in turn, decided to run for governor again as an independent, expecting to pick up support from disaffected Republicans and Federalists.

The Republican candidate was New York Supreme Court justice Morgan Lewis, who was affiliated with Governor Clinton and the Jeffersonians. Betraying their utter disarray, the Federalists did not even run their own candidate. Hamilton's failure to find a viable Federalist surely amused Burr. "Hamilton is intriguing for any candidate who can have a chance of success against Aaron Burr," he confided to his daughter Theodosia, referring to himself in the third person. Much to Hamilton's chagrin, many prominent Federalists, including former Supreme Court chief justice and New York governor John Jay, signed on with Burr. Hamilton maintained a public position of neutrality, while opposing Burr with all his might in private.

Over the years Hamilton had compiled a long list of reasons that Burr was unfit for office. Now there was a fresh one: the suspicion that Burr might be secretly scheming to create a new country out of New England and New York.

This preposterous-sounding proposition was not a product of Hamilton's imagination. Some New England Federalists sorely begrudged their loss of power and they didn't much like the idea of being under the thumb of Virginia, by far the largest state. They were terrified that the Louisiana Purchase—Jefferson's massive 1803 land deal—would lead to new slaveholding states and further diminish their power. (That concern proved all too true.) This group of schemers were trying to drum up interest in a Northern Confederacy that would be "exempt from the...corrupting influence and oppression" of Jefferson, Madison, and other southern Republicans. When they sounded out Burr, he was typically enigmatic, suggesting that he was sympathetic to their concerns, but unwilling to commit himself to their cause. Hamilton, though, feared that Burr would jump at the chance to head up a Northern Confederacy, and would use the New York governorship as a stepping-stone to that goal. "A dismemberment of the Union is likely to be one of the first fruits of his elevation," he wrote. As an immigrant who had adopted America as his own nation, Hamilton was unalterably opposed to breaking apart the country he had worked so hard to create. "I view the suggestion of such a project with horror."

As the campaign progressed, the drumbeat of Republican attacks on Burr increased. Rarely had political accusations plunged so far into the gutter. Editor Cheetham's *American Citizen* assembled a list of "upwards of twenty women of ill fame" whom Burr had supposedly sported with, even printing their initials in the paper. Cheetham also imagined a lurid "nigger ball" at Burr's Richmond Hill mansion, supposedly organized to woo black voters, where Burr had allegedly danced with and seduced a voluptuous black woman. He kept goading Burr with Hamilton's past attacks, printing that Hamilton had opposed Burr "BECAUSE HE HAD NO PRINCIPLE, either in morals or in politics." Those were indeed sentiments Hamilton had expressed in the past, and continued to express privately.

Burr could hardly fail to take notice of the inflammatory words. A piece of Burr's own campaign literature offers a clue to how much they stung. "Colonel Burr has been loaded with almost every epithet of abuse to be found in the English language. He has been represented as a man totally destitute of political principle or integrity."

We cannot know for certain whether Burr believed that such slurs came directly from Hamilton's pen, but he certainly knew that they accurately reflected Hamilton's feelings.

The 1804 New York gubernatorial election was held in late April. Burr narrowly won New York City, but was trounced statewide, receiving only 40 percent of the vote. Many Federalists had voted for him, but not nearly enough. No longer vice president, his bid for governor dashed, Burr's political fortunes had crashed and burned. Meanwhile, his financial debt continued to pile up. He affected bravado, but in fact he was enraged and looking for someone to blame. A few months earlier he had told a friend that he would "call out the first man of any respectability" that he discovered to be behind the "infamous" slanderings. He proved true to his word.

Charles Cooper was a doctor, a lawyer, and a Republican politician living in Albany, New York. Back in March 1804 he had been seated at a dinner party where the conversation turned toward the election for governor. The wine flowed, and tongues loosened. One of the other guests was Alexander Hamilton, who had a few choice comments on the subject of Aaron Burr.

Cooper supported Morgan Lewis, the Republican candidate, and apparently saw an opportunity to damage Burr. He wrote a letter about the dinner, saying he had heard Hamilton say he considered Burr "a dangerous man and one not to be trusted." Further, Cooper added, "I could detail to you a still more despicable opinion which General Hamilton has expressed of Mr. Burr." By accident, or design, this letter was published in an Albany newspaper during the final days of the election campaign. Some weeks later, a copy of the newspaper fell into Burr's hands. The phrase "a still more despicable opinion" deeply rankled. Once again Hamilton seemed to be behind an attack that called into question Burr's integrity. Something snapped. Burr had finally had enough.

As the *Philadelphia Aurora* once wrote, "While other men are debating, he resolves, and while they resolve, he acts."

June 18, 1804: Twenty-three days left

A Monday morning with fine June weather. Not a cloud in the sky. Alexander Hamilton was hard at work in his New York law office when attorney and Burr confidant William Van Ness came to call. He brought with him a letter from Aaron Burr, and asked Hamilton to read it.

Sir,

I send for your perusal a letter signed Charles D. Cooper, which, though apparently published some time ago, has but very recently come to my knowledge. Mr. Van Ness, who does me the favor to deliver this, will point out to you that clause of the letter to which I particularly request your attention.

You must perceive, Sir, the necessity of a prompt and unqual-ified acknowledgement or denial of the use of any expression which would warrant the assertions of Dr. Cooper.

I have the honor to be,

Your obedient servant
A. Burr

As Hamilton perused the note, he immediately understood that Burr was issuing an ultimatum, and he would have to respond.

This was an extraordinary moment, unparalleled in American history. The sitting vice president of the United States was initiating a challenge to the former secretary of the treasury that was highly likely to end in a duel. This would not be some private exchange of shots; it could be nothing less than a momentous affair that would rock the still-new nation.

What was on Burr's mind at this moment? The best answer comes from Burr himself, in words he wrote to a friend one week after the duel to justify his actions. Hamilton, he complained, had "long indulged himself" in saying "improper and offensive" things about Burr's character.

On two different occasions...having reason to apprehend that he had gone so far as to afford me fair occasion for calling on him [i.e., challenging him to a duel] he anticipated me by coming forward voluntarily and making apologies and concessions. From delicacy to him and from a sincere desire for peace, I have never mentioned these circumstances, always hoping that the generosity of my conduct would have had some influence on him. In this I have been constantly deceived, and it became impossible that I could consistently with self-respect again forbear.

Clearly Burr's exasperation went far beyond this one note. He had endured a tidal wave of abuse from Hamilton without responding. His anger ran cold and deep. There needed to be a reckoning. Beyond that, Burr was almost certainly making a political calculation as well.

Hamilton was an unyielding foe, single-handedly blocking him from gaining further Federalist support. If he could take Hamilton down a notch or remove him from the scene, it might open up new avenues for Burr's political forays.

At that time, it was not uncommon for defeated politicians to use dueling as a means of recouping their standing, though many disapproved of the practice. Thomas Jefferson and John Adams, for example, both opposed dueling for any reason. Tellingly, neither man had served in the military, where dueling flourished. Burr and Hamilton had both been officers on the battlefield, and both had been immersed in the military culture that emphasized the importance of courage, coolness under fire, and defending one's honor. Neither would hesitate if they believed honor required them to take part.

June 20, 1804: Twenty-one days left

Hamilton waited two days before sending Burr a lengthy response. This is how it began.

> Sir,
>   I have maturely reflected on the subject of your letter of the 18th inst. And the more I have reflected the more I have become convinced, that I could not, without manifest impropriety, make the avowal or disavowal which you think necessary.

Hamilton's letter was full of legalistic nitpicking. Since Burr had not specified what remark he found upsetting, Hamilton claimed he had no way to take it back. Hamilton's tone was mocking and sarcastic. He seemed to be toying with Burr.

'Tis evident that the phrase, "Still more despicable" admits of infinite shades, from very light to very dark. How am I to judge of the degree intended? Or how shall I annex any precise idea to language so indefinite?

He split hairs on the difference between "despicable" and "more despicable," and concluded by saying he simply could not respond to anything so vague.

If Hamilton had simply responded that he said nothing at the dinner fitting Dr. Cooper's description, and apologized for anything that might have been taken in that way, it might have sufficed to meet the demands of honor and preclude the need for a duel. Hamilton, however, was not willing to give even that small degree of satisfaction to a man he had publicly castigated and privately disdained for so long. For Hamilton, too, there was a political dimension. Burr, he felt, still represented a threat to the nation. Standing up to him in a very public duel might thwart Burr's ambitions, which Hamilton viewed as nefarious.

June 21, 1804: Twenty days left

Burr's response came the next day, a Friday. No surprise: Hamilton's note inflamed him even further. "I regret to find in it nothing of that sincerity and delicacy which you profess to value." Then he indulged in some lecturing of his own. "Political opposition can never absolve gentlemen from the necessity of a rigid adherence to the laws of honor, and the rules of decorum." The issue, said Burr, had nothing to do with the "grammatical accuracy" of Cooper's letter, but its content. Had Hamilton been "uttering expressions or opinions derogatory to my honor"?

Van Ness brought Burr's letter to Hamilton. After reading it, Hamilton looked up from his desk and told Van News that he considered it "rude and offensive" and that "Mr. Burr must take such steps as he might think proper." In the language of the day, that meant a duel was imminent—unless Burr wanted to back down.

June 22, 1804: Nineteen days left

Clouds filled the sky over Manhattan this Saturday, as the two antagonists closeted themselves with the men who would become their seconds. In Burr's case that was William Van Ness, who had been shuttling the letters back and forth. Burr took the opportunity to vent his anger. The fact that Hamilton considered him a political adversary simply did not justify the petty personal attacks that Hamilton had hurled at him. In Burr's mind, such a rivalry demanded "greater delicacy." He believed it appropriate to speak of a rival only in terms of respect, "to do justice to his merits, to be silent of his foibles." That, he said, was the way he had always behaved toward Jay, Adams, and Hamilton, the only three men who could be considered his rivals.

Hamilton, he said bitterly, had obsessively taken the opposite tack. "His name has been lent to the support of base slanders [that] he has never had the generosity, the magnanimity or the candor to contradict or disavow." Burr told Van Ness he was obliged to conclude that there was a "settled and implacable malevolence" on the part of Hamilton and that he would "never cease in his conduct." Therefore, said Burr, he had no choice but to stand by his challenge.

Hamilton paid a call on his friend and fellow attorney Nathaniel Pendleton and filled him in. Pendleton offered to negotiate, in much the same way Burr had negotiated in the quarrel between Hamilton and Monroe five years before. After consulting Pendleton, Hamilton headed uptown to spend the rest of the weekend at The Grange.

June 23, 1804: Eighteen days left

Burr put the exchange with Hamilton out of his mind. He hosted a party at Richmond Hill to celebrate his daughter's birthday, even though she was hundreds of miles away in South Carolina. It was an evening filled with laughter, dancing, and toasts to Theodosia's health, with no hint of what was unfolding.

June 26, 1804: Fifteen days left

The two seconds put their heads together. They came up with a plan to defuse the situation. Burr would write a letter inquiring whether Hamilton had said anything that night to Dr. Cooper that attributed "dishonorable conduct" to Burr or impugned his private character. If the question were posed that way, Hamilton could respond that to the "best of his recollection [the conversation] consisted of comments on the political principles and views of Colonel Burr...without reference to any particular instance of past conduct, or to private character."

It just wasn't enough for Burr. His blood was boiling. He felt the proposal was "fraught with ambiguity" that made it "insidious and insulting." By focusing on that one conversation, he believed Hamilton was angling to evade responsibility for other attacks on Burr's character. "These things must have an end," Burr exclaimed. Now it was his turn to parse language and take offense. He assumed from Cooper's original letter that Hamilton had indeed disparaged him at other times—unless Hamilton would avow that he had not. If Hamilton denied a conversation on that one particular day, said Burr, "the world may say 'true, but the day anterior or the day subsequent such things were said by Genl. H.' and this would indeed be a fair inference from such partial negation." Burr wouldn't settle for anything less than a general denial that Hamilton had ever said anything "derogatory to Burr's character."

Hamilton's second, Nathaniel Pendleton, replied that Hamilton flatly refused to respond regarding every word he had ever said about Burr. Furthermore, he passed on Hamilton's accusation that Burr was displaying "predetermined hostility" toward him. Burr indignantly denied it.

The insurmountable truth, of course, was that Hamilton was guilty as charged. He had said many, many things impugning Burr's private character, his morals, and his financial profligacy over the last decade. There was no way to take it all back wholesale. If he offered some sort of blanket apology or softening of his remarks, it would mark him as a laughingstock or, worse, a coward unwilling to stand up for his own strongly held opinions of his political foe. Not to mention that such a denial would be totally false. Whatever his faults, Hamilton "disdained concealment," as his friend Gouverneur Morris put it. He was not willing to lie to save himself from a confrontation.

June 27, 1804: Fourteen days left

The letters and meetings between the two camps had gone on for a week, each accusing the other of rudeness, defiance, evasiveness, and dissembling. The time for talk was done. Van Ness passed along

Burr's explicit challenge to a duel. Hamilton accepted it, but requested a delay so that he might finish up his cases still pending in court. The die was cast, but the conflict was put on ice for two weeks.

July 3, 1804: Eight days left

Hamilton did not confide in his wife Eliza. He carried on with his court cases and a busy social calendar. On this night, he and Eliza held a gala dinner party at The Grange with more than seventy guests. Notably, they included William Short, a Jefferson protégé; and Abigail Adams Smith, the daughter of John and Abigail Adams, along with her husband.

July 4, 1804: Seven days left

Burr and Hamilton both attended the Society of the Cincinnati dinner at Fraunces Tavern. Observers marked the difference in their moods. Hamilton was the life of the party. Burr was silent and sour. In fact, now that he had committed to the duel, Burr was becoming impatient. "I should with regret pass over another day," he wrote a few days later to Van Ness. Finally, it was agreed that the duel would take place on the morning of Wednesday, July 11. Burr was not happy with the early-morning hour, but agreed to it anyway. "Anything, so we but get on!" he responded. As the person being challenged, Hamilton had choice of weapons. He picked the ornate dueling pistols owned by his brother-in-law John Barker Church—a macabre choice, indeed, given their role in his son's death.

On this same day, Hamilton composed a farewell letter to his wife Eliza to be opened in case of his death.

July 9, 1804: Two days left

On the Monday before the duel, Hamilton prepared his last will and testament. That may also be the day he composed a "Statement on Impending Duel with Aaron Burr." True to form, Hamilton wanted to defend himself in writing, in case he did not survive the encounter. He said that he was "desirous of avoiding this interview[6] for many reasons." Those reasons included his opposition to dueling, love for his wife and children, concern about his creditors, and the fact that he felt "no ill-will to Colonel Burr, distinct from political opposition." Yet he had made "very unfavorable criticisms" of Burr, and an apology was "out of the question." He acknowledged that he felt he must go through with the duel to uphold his reputation. He could not withdraw because it would destroy his "ability to be useful . . . in those crises of public affairs which seem likely to happen."

While Hamilton wrote that he thought Burr had been "menacing" and "offensive," he added that it was not his purpose "to affix any odium on the conduct of Colonel Burr." He said that he hoped he was wrong about Burr, that he hoped "that he by his future conduct may show himself worthy of all confidence and esteem, and prove an ornament and blessing to his country." Recognizing that he might have injured Burr with his comments, Hamilton wrote, it was his intention "to *reserve* and *throw away* my first fire, and I *have thoughts* even of *reserving* my second fire—and thus giving a double opportunity to Colonel Burr to pause and to reflect." Of course, in writing the letter, Hamilton knew the words would only be read if he died. He could change his mind and then throw away the letter if

---

6. "Interview" was a commonly used euphemism for a duel.

he survived. He also told his second, Nathaniel Pendleton, and other trusted friends, that he would not fire at Burr—a fact that Burr had no way of knowing.

July 10, 1804: One day left

The day before the duel, Hamilton penned his last political letter. He wrote to Massachusetts Federalist Theodore Sedgwick, "I will here express but one sentiment, which is, that dismemberment of our Empire will be a clear sacrifice of great positive advantages, without any counterbalancing good." To the very end, he was concerned about the nation he had helped to shape.

Hamilton spent the night before the duel in his house in the city. Eliza and most of the children were up at The Grange. Around 10 P.M., Hamilton wrote a short note to be delivered to her in the event of his death. He reiterated that he was not going to fire first, and explained why. "The Scruples of a Christian have determined me to expose my own life to any extent rather than subject myself to the guilt of taking the life of another. This must increase my hazards & redoubles my pangs for you. But you had rather I should die innocent than live guilty." After writing these words, which he knew might be his last communication with his wife, he turned in for a few hours of sleep.

Historians have pored over the words Hamilton wrote in his final days, trying to peer into his mind to see if he was depressed or suicidal. Why else would a man with a loving wife and seven children who depended on him be willing to gamble his life this way? Clearly he understood that he might face certain death in the morning. Yet there is nothing to suggest that he yearned for the grave.

Burr spent the final night before the duel at Richmond Hill. He too wrote out letters to be delivered if he was killed in the morning. He asked his daughter Theodosia to burn all of his correspondence that might "injure any person. This is more particularly applicable to the letters of my female correspondents." He specified particular bundles of letters that should go in the fire. He gave her several other instructions to be carried out in case of his death, and closed with these words: "I am indebted to you, my dearest Theodosia, for a very great portion of the happiness which I have enjoyed in this life." He also wrote to her husband, Joseph Alston. "If it should be my lot to fall . . . I commit to you all that is most dear to me—my reputation and my daughter."

There were stories later that Burr spent the final days practicing with his pistol, said to be indicative of his murderous intent. His friends adamantly denied that. In any case, he fell asleep on the couch and slept soundly, untroubled by any concerns of what fate might await him the following day.

ONE

ENCOUNTER IN WEEHAWKEN

Zero Hour

Sometime just before 7:30 on the morning of Wednesday, July 11, 1804, the actors finally took their places for the climactic scene of the drama. The vice president of the United States faced the former secretary of the treasury on the dueling ground in Weehawken, New Jersey, across the Hudson from New York City. The spot was a secluded one—what happened here could only be observed by the duelists and their seconds.

Hamilton finally finished fiddling with his glasses. He and Burr now faced each other from thirty feet apart, loaded pistols in hand. The two seconds, Van Ness and Pendleton, stood off to the side. Dr. David Hosack, Hamilton's personal physician, remained down by the boats so he would not see things he might be called upon to testify about later. The sun was climbing fast into the sky and a cool breeze off the water hinted at the beautiful day to come. Pendleton checked one last time to make sure both men were ready. Then he shouted "Present!" The moment had arrived.

Burr fired first. That's for certain. No, Hamilton fired first. There can be no doubt. The shots came at nearly the same time. No, no, no, the shots were three to four seconds apart.

Four people witnessed what happened in the next few seconds, one of whom was mortally wounded during that period. From their accounts came two different versions of the story that are nearly impossible to reconcile. What is known for certain is this:

When Aaron Burr pulled the trigger on the ornate Wogdon dueling pistol in his right hand, it sparked an explosion that propelled a .54-caliber lead ball out the muzzle at a speed of approximately 545 miles per hour. The ball, weighing less than an ounce, traversed the thirty feet between Burr and Hamilton in less than one-twentieth of a second, imperceptibly slowing down as the distance flew by. It tore through Hamilton's waistcoat and shirt, ripped through the skin into his abdomen, then glanced off a rib. Traveling in a new direction now, it plowed remorselessly through his liver, causing irrevocable damage before lodging in one of his vertebrae.

The ball from Hamilton's pistol went wide of the mark, hitting the limb of a cedar tree about twelve feet high, and four feet to the right of the line between Hamilton and Burr.

Who fired first? Was it Burr, the remorseless murderer bent on gunning down the man who had galled him for so long? Or was it Hamilton, hypocritically ignoring his stated intention to reserve his fire?

Burr's second, William Van Ness, stated unequivocally that Hamilton fired first. "After a few seconds of time, Colonel Burr fired; and instantly General Hamilton fell." Van Ness was particularly adamant that several seconds passed after Hamilton's shot before Burr pulled the trigger. Burr said he saw Hamilton take aim and fire "very promptly," and that he didn't return fire for two to three seconds. Van Ness later asked Burr why he had waited so long. "He answered that the smoke of Mr. Hamilton's pistol for a moment obscured his sight."

This is completely at odds with the account of Nathaniel Pendleton, Hamilton's second. "General Hamilton did not fire first, and . . . he did not fire at all *at Colonel Burr*." In Pendleton's version of events, Burr fired first, and Hamilton's pistol went off an instant later, most likely a reflex reaction, exactly the same thing that had happened with his son three years earlier. Pendleton buttressed this observation by reporting what Hamilton had told him the night before: "He had made up his mind *not to fire at Colonel Burr the first time, but to receive his fire, and fire in the air.*" As they rowed the mortally wounded Hamilton back to Manhattan, Pendleton said that Hamilton warned him to be careful with his pistol, because it had not been discharged—suggesting that he was unaware he had even fired.

Burr and Van Ness scoffed at this account. Burr didn't think Pendleton was much of a witness. After Hamilton fell, he said, Pendleton appeared "a good deal agitated and not to be in a true state of mind suitable for observing with accuracy what passed." Van Ness was even more harsh in his response. "As to the pretense that General Hamilton did not intend to fire and that Colonel Burr knew it, it is more dishonorable to the deceased than the survivor."

Is there any way to reconcile the two accounts, along with Hamilton's expressed avowal that he was going to reserve his fire? Possibly, but there is another fact that needs to be put into evidence first. The pistols were each fitted with a hair trigger, a fact known to Hamilton but not to Burr. When a secret spring was set, the slightest pressure on the trigger would cause the pistol to go off. This might conceivably give Hamilton an advantage in the duel. Burr partisans over the years have pointed to this as an example of Hamiltonian duplicity. According to Pendleton, however, when he asked Hamilton if he should set the hair trigger, Hamilton responded, "Not this time."

But what if it *was* set—by accident or on purpose? (People sometimes lie, after all.) It is possible that as Hamilton brought the pistol up from his side, he fired it unintentionally. That would account for the wild shot. After watching Hamilton sight his pistol and fidget with his glasses moments before, Burr could not doubt that such a shot was meant to kill. In the heat of the adrenaline-charged moment, firing back would be an almost instinctive response. If that is what actually happened, it means that Hamilton remained true to his vow, and Burr did not murder Hamilton in cold blood. Of course, that is just a theory, no more or less likely than many others. More than two centuries after the fact, it is impossible to know exactly what happened. Strongly held opinions about who fired first (and thus who should be blamed) tend to reflect the observer's respective opinions of the two men, rather than a careful sifting of the evidence.

Shots fired. Boom. Boom. Action, reaction. Hamilton slumped to the ground. Burr heard him moan, "I am a dead man." Seeing Hamilton prostrate, Burr took a step toward him. It seemed to Pendleton as if a flash of regret crossed his face. Van Ness quickly guided Burr down toward the riverbank, using an umbrella to shield his face from Dr. Hosack and Hamilton's boatmen, who were now climbing up to the duel site. Halfway down, an agitated Burr tried to go back. "I must speak with him," he said. But Van Ness hustled him to their boat and they rowed back across the Hudson. Burr returned to Richmond Hill, where he awaited news on Hamilton's fate.

Dr. Hosack found Hamilton sprawled on the ground, being cradled by Pendleton. "This is a mortal wound, doctor," Hamilton said, before passing out. After a quick examination, Hosack "considered him as irrecoverably gone." He and Pendleton carried Hamilton to the boat, where he regained consciousness. He told them he could no longer feel his lower extremities, and as they approached the New York shore, he begged them to send for his wife.

A friend of Hamilton's, William Bayard, was waiting by the dock— he had heard from a servant that Hamilton had headed across the Hudson early in the morning, and guessed what it was about. He had Hamilton brought to his house and carried to a large upstairs bedroom. There Hamilton was able to sip some wine and water, and was given laudanum, a painkiller. When Eliza arrived, she became consumed with "frantic grief" that tore at the hearts of those present. "It has been but two years [sic] since her son was killed in the same manner," said a family friend. "Gracious God! What must be her feelings?" Hamilton tried to calm her by saying, "Remember, Eliza, you are a Christian." Others gathered to keep vigil. Angelica Schuyler Church was there, "weeping her heart out" in the words of Gouverneur Morris, now a U.S. senator from New York, and also attending to the death of his friend.

Hamilton wished to take communion before he died. Episcopal

Bishop Benjamin Moore was reluctant to offer it because of Hamilton's involvement in a duel, as well as the fact that he was not a regular churchgoer, but he eventually relented.

Word of the duel spread through New York City. Business ground to a halt and people talked of little else. "General Hamilton is still alive but no hopes of his recovery," noted diarist Elizabeth De Hart Bleecker the following morning, Thursday, July 12. At about the same hour, Aaron Burr wrote to Dr. Hosack, asking about "the present state of General Hamilton and the hopes which are entertained of his recovery." Stories later circulated that Burr was nonchalant about Hamilton's fate, even joked about it. Van Ness denied this. "Far from exhibiting any degree of levity or expressing any satisfaction at the result of the meeting," he said, Burr's response was one of "regret and concern."

The French consul-general showed up and offered the assistance of surgeons serving aboard French warships in the harbor. They examined Hamilton and confirmed that there was no hope. Eliza brought in the children, and lined up all seven of them by the bed so Hamilton could see them one last time. She lifted two-year-old Philip, so his father could give him a brief kiss. As death drew near, Hamilton's "mind retained all its usual strength and composure," according to Dr. Hosack. At two in the afternoon, Alexander Hamilton died of his wounds, six months shy of his fiftieth birthday.

As the news of his death spread across the city, church sextons trudged up the narrow stairs of their steeples to strap leather muffles to the clappers of their giant bells. These were designed to dampen the sound. Soon the mournful tones of muffled church bells began to toll in honor of the fallen Hamilton.

Perhaps it was that day, or the next, that Eliza Hamilton was given the packet Hamilton had prepared for her. It included the letter of farewell penned a week before. "If it had been possible for me to have avoided the interview," he wrote, "my love for you and my precious children would have been alone a decisive motive. But it was not possible without sacrifices which would have rendered me unworthy of your esteem." He closed with these words: "Adieu best of wives and best of women. Embrace all my darling children for me."

With a single shot, Aaron Burr transformed Alexander Hamilton from a tarnished politician into a beloved martyr. Flowery tributes to the fallen Hamilton filled the New York newspapers. "Thus has perished, by an untimely death, a patriot of exalted merit, a soldier and a civilian of pre-eminent worth," thundered the *New York Gazette*. "Thus has America been bereft of her second Washington!" The *Mercantile Advertiser* praised Hamilton as the man "whose transcendental talents, and unwearied efforts, contributed essentially to the erection of our national fabric." Many noted Hamilton's relative youth. Like the assassination of John F. Kennedy 150 years later, Hamilton's death seemed even more tragic because he was cut down in the prime of life. He died "in the midst of his usefulness" said the *New York Evening Post*.

As word spread that Hamilton had vowed to reserve his fire, and that Nathaniel Pendleton was vigorously asserting he had indeed done just that, Burr found himself speedily vilified. James Cheetham's *American Citizen,* once again taking up the cudgel against Burr, proclaimed that Hamilton's death was the result of "a long meditated and predetermined system of hostility on the part of Mr. Burr and his confidential advisers." The *Mercantile Advertiser* berated Burr for taking "cool and deadly aim against the first citizen of our country, the father of a numerous family." A New York coroner's jury indicted Burr for murder, accusing him, in the chilling traditional phrase of the time, of "not having the fear of God before his eyes, but being moved and seduced by the instigation of the devil." New Jersey indicted Burr as well, though neither charge went anywhere.

"The most abominable falsehoods are current and have issued from the house where Hamilton now lies," complained Burr the day after Hamilton's death, stunned to find himself under attack. He rallied friends to his defense, but to little avail. To Burr's mind (and there was a great deal of truth to this), supporters of Hamilton and Jefferson were joining forces against him. They "unite in endeavoring to excite public sympathy in [Hamilton's] favor and indignation against his antagonist," he wrote to his son-in-law, Joseph Alston. A few days later he remarked that the duel "has driven me into a sort of exile and may terminate in an actual and permanent ostracism." He found it bitterly amusing that Republicans "who have been for years invoking Hamilton as a disgrace to the country and a pest to society are now the most vehement in his praise, and you will readily perceive that their motive is not respect to him, but malice to me." He soon decided it was prudent to leave New York before he was arrested or lynched, and slipped out of town.

Burr was not the only one to see political motives behind the sudden canonization of Hamilton. "You will readily understand the different uses to which the event is turned," wrote James Madison to James Monroe. Treasury Secretary Albert Gallatin, in New York at the time of the duel, decried the "artificial feeling or semblance of feeling" whipped up by Federalists opposed to the Jefferson administration.

Ironically, it was Jefferson, enemy to both men, who benefited the most from their duel. His greatest critic had been silenced and his most dangerous rival politically neutralized. Jefferson himself refrained from comment. Later that summer, Lafayette wrote Jefferson in despair over the death of his old comrade-in-arms. "The deplorable fate of my friend Hamilton has deeply afflicted me—I am sure that whatever have been the differences of parties, you have ever been sensible of his merits, and now feel for his loss." In fact, Jefferson's papers contain neither expressions of grief nor any reflections about Hamilton's passing. The killing left this cool character utterly unmoved.

John Adams was another who chose not to raise his voice in tribute to Hamilton. His wife Abigail wrote a friend that she did not rejoice in Hamilton's fall, but she went on to gently mock the widespread lamentations over his death. "I believe the seasons will perform their annual round though Hamilton sleeps in the grave, and that should pressing occasion call for heroes and statesmen and patriots, we shall find them springing into life and activity as we have before."

All business in New York was officially suspended on the day of Alexander Hamilton's funeral. From a population of twelve thousand at the time Hamilton moved there in 1783, the city had grown to a bustling metropolis of sixty thousand, partially as a result of the commercial and financial policies put in place by the deceased. On this day it seemed as if the entire population turned out to mourn him. Muffled bells began to toll at 6 A.M., and kept ringing for hour upon hour. At noon the funeral procession left the house of John Barker Church, where Hamilton's body lay, and slowly began the funeral procession to Trinity Church. Crowds lined the streets, spectators gawked from windows, and a few hardy souls climbed trees to catch a view. An artillery unit, a militia unit, and aged Revolutionary War officers from the Society of the Cincinnati led the way. On top of Hamilton's coffin lay his general's hat and sword. His gray horse was dressed in mourning, with empty boots reversed in the stirrups, a military tradition going back centuries. The horse "was led by two black servants dressed in white, and white turbans trimmed with black" according to the *New York Evening Post.* "It was one of the purest and most affecting processions ever witnessed in this place," wrote Elizabeth De Hart Bleecker.

Flanked by four of Hamilton's sons, Gouverneur Morris gave the funeral oration from a stage erected at Trinity Church. In a diary entry he wrote the night before, he fretted about what to say, acknowledging that he needed to steer clear of Hamilton's many flaws, including the fact that he was "indiscreet, vain and opinionated." Morris came through with an emotional eulogy that asked people not to forget Hamilton's many accomplishments. "I charge you to protect his fame—it is all he has left." He also held Hamilton up as an example to future generations, suggesting that when in doubt about a particular course of action, people should ask, "Would Hamilton have done this thing?"

Hamilton was laid to rest in the small burial ground adjacent to the church. An honor guard fired three volleys over the grave. Merchant vessels in the harbor lowered their colors to half-mast. French and British navy ships were decked out in mourning and fired forty-eight-gun salutes. "We never witnessed, in this country or in Europe on any similar occasion, so general a sorrow, such an universal regret or a ceremonial [sic] more awful and impressive," wrote the *Mercantile Advertiser.*

Aaron Burr made his way south. He reconnected with an old flame in Philadelphia, and wrote a saucy note about it to his daughter. "If any male friend of yours should be dying of ennui, recommend him to engage in a duel and a courtship at the same time." He visited South Carolina and Georgia. In some places he was greeted almost as a hero for shooting Hamilton.

Even though Jefferson had picked George Clinton as his running mate in the forthcoming election, Aaron Burr was still vice president. By the time the Senate reconvened in November, the hubbub had begun to die down, and Burr returned to Washington to preside over its sessions. He earned praise for the way he chaired the impeachment trial of Supreme Court justice Samuel Chase, a Federalist, who was acquitted. When Burr's term was over, he headed west, and into a new controversy.

Less than a month after the duel, Vice President Burr reached out to British Ambassador Anthony Merry with an amazing offer to help separate the western United States from the rest of the country. Merry believed Burr was motivated by "his great ambition and spirit of revenge" against Jefferson. This was the beginning of a shadowy conspiracy comprising Burr and General James Wilkinson, which may have involved leading an armed uprising to create an independent country, or possibly to take Mexico from Spain, or maybe even to collaborate with Spain to capture Washington. There is much about this extraordinary cabal that remains murky. Burr was raising troops for a military expedition of some sort when Wilkinson turned against him, and reported the plot to the White House. In 1807 Thomas Jefferson directed that Burr be arrested and tried for treason. At the sensational trial that followed, Chief Justice John Marshall, a longtime enemy of Jefferson, acquitted Burr on lack of evidence. Nevertheless, Burr's political career was finally and irrevocably demolished. He spent four years in self-imposed exile in Great Britain, then returned to New York, where he lived quietly the last twenty-five years of his life. In 1834 he married a wealthy widow named Eliza Jumel, but divorced soon afterward, and died in 1836.

Eliza Hamilton survived her husband by fifty years, dying at age ninety-seven in 1854. She founded New York City's first orphanage in honor of her orphan husband, and spent much of her time preserving and accumulating letters, testimonials, and other documents defending his reputation against the aspersions of Jeffersonians. All of her surviving children lived to great age, many to their eighties and nineties. One son, James Hamilton, became acting secretary of state under Andrew Jackson. Another, John Church Hamilton, wrote a seven-volume biography of his father, based on the papers preserved by his mother. And a third, Alexander Hamilton Jr., represented Eliza Jumel in her divorce from Aaron Burr. More than two decades after Hamilton's death, the two men's lives remained intertwined.

Late in life, Aaron Burr is said to have been reading the humorous novel *Tristram Shandy* by Laurence Sterne, when he made the following observation: "Had I read Sterne more and Voltaire less, I should have known the world was wide enough for Hamilton and me."

EPILOGUE

A quarter of a century after the death of Alexander Hamilton, his son James had an unexpected encounter with Albert Gallatin, who had served as secretary of the treasury under Jefferson and Madison. Gallatin related that when he first took over the Treasury Department, Jefferson directed him to go through all the accounts to unearth evidence of Hamilton's corruption, as well as any flaws in Hamilton's financial system that the Federalists had been covering up. No friend of the Federalists (who had once kicked him out of the Senate for trumped-up reasons relating to his Swiss birth), Gallatin approached the task with relish, convinced that there was much to discover.

Some time later, when he reported back to the president, Jefferson pressed Gallatin with some eagerness about what he had found. "I have found the most perfect system ever formed," Gallatin reportedly replied. "Any change that should be made in it would injure it. Hamilton made no blunders, committed no frauds. He did nothing wrong."

Finishing up the story, Gallatin concluded: "I think Mr. Jefferson was disappointed."

In judging the two rivals, posterity has clearly rendered its verdict in favor of the man whose face appears on the $10 bill. (He and

Benjamin Franklin are the only two nonpresidents who appear on U.S. currency.) He has even become a Broadway star. His myriad achievements are so numerous they almost defy cataloging. Burr, on the other hand, is remembered for little else than shooting Hamilton. Over the years, he has joined Benedict Arnold as one of the twin villains of American history.

And yet...

In their fatal showdown, Burr was the challenger, but he was certainly provoked. Not just on one occasion, but many times. Even Hamilton himself, in his final writings, grudgingly admitted that it was possible he had done injury to Burr. That, he said, was why he was going to reserve his shot.

Burr was excoriated for killing someone in a duel. President Andrew Jackson, however, killed at least one man in a duel, and sustained a chest wound in another, yet still managed to be elected president. Burr clearly chose the wrong target.

Burr's alleged plot to create a new country with himself at the head is frequently cited as evidence of his treachery, and it is pretty damning. But how different is what he did from the actions of Federalists in New England who plotted secession in 1804, and again during the war of 1812; or what Sam Houston and others did in Texas a couple of decades hence; or, for that matter, what Jefferson Davis, Robert E. Lee, and a few million other Southerners did in 1861? Yet those people are still honored.

Of course, Burr started with a few of strikes against him. As a man in the middle, never rabidly loyal to a political party, he lacked partisans to argue his cause. His only daughter, Theodosia, died in 1813, so she wasn't there to advocate for him, either. Cautious about committing himself in writing, careful about culling his records, Burr left a comparatively paltry selection of papers. That makes it hard for historians disposed to argue his case. By comparison, Alexander Hamilton's papers, when eventually published, ran to twenty-six volumes. And he was survived by a wife and seven children who kept his memory alive.

Alexander Hamilton viewed politics as a sacred mission, a calling, a quest. He fought passionately, sometimes excessively, to harness a vision of what he thought America could be. Aaron Burr saw politics as a career, like the law, in which he hoped to excel and advance as far as possible. In that regard he was not unlike a great many people in politics today. He approached the whole business with a more dispassionate eye than Hamilton. His interest in the nuts and bolts of electioneering led to innovations that remain a staple of modern campaigning.

There is an ironic twist to the two men's politics that is often overlooked. Born in poverty, Hamilton came to fear the mob, the "levelers," and favored a government of elites. Born into the country's aristocracy, Burr championed an expansion of the voting franchise and the rights of immigrants.

When Hamilton looked at Burr, he saw a man with no fixed ideology other than winning. When Burr looked at Hamilton, he saw a fanatic warped by zealotry. The years magnified these perceived character traits until the two rivals could see little else.

What might Hamilton have accomplished if he had survived the duel? He was only forty-nine at the time of his death. True, his career was at a low ebb in 1804, but many other politicians, from Winston Churchill to Richard Nixon, have risen from the ashes after their careers were pronounced dead.

Did he harbor presidential ambitions? It was not a subject he talked about, but it is hard to believe it never crossed his mind. He was not disqualified by his birth in the West Indies. As a citizen of New York (and hence the United States) at the time the Constitution was adopted, Hamilton could have run for president once he turned thirty-five. He would have been eligible to run in 1796, but the sitting vice president, John Adams, was the obvious Federalist candidate to succeed Washington. Hamilton might have considered running four years later, had he not been tarnished by the "Reynolds Pamphlet." If he had lived, it is difficult to imagine him standing on the sidelines while a procession of Federalist candidates were ground into the dust by his old Virginia foes: Jefferson, Madison, and Monroe. Still, it is possible that the self-confidence of this immigrant didn't extend quite that far, that he saw himself as the loyal aide to a great man, rather than a great man himself.

And what of Burr? Would he still have involved himself in his desperate western conspiracy if he had not been ostracized and reviled following the duel? Or might he have bided his time, hoarded his resources, and waited to fight another day? It is possible he could have resurrected his career, running for governor, or senator, or maybe even one day for president against Alexander Hamilton.

We will never know.

★ ★ ★

Two centuries have obliterated most traces of Hamilton and Burr in and around New York City. The battlefield where they fought the

British is covered by pavement and tall buildings. The courtrooms where they argued have long since been replaced by newer ones. Many of their residences have been torn down. The dueling ground at Weehawken is now a rail yard, although a monument at the top of the cliff commemorates the event.

Vestiges of their lives do remain. Though the palatial Richmond Hill is long gone, Hamilton's country home, The Grange, still stands in Harlem, despite having been moved twice. Hamilton's stately grave lies behind Trinity Church, steps from Broadway. Two businesses launched by Hamilton, the Bank of New York (now BNY Mellon) and the *New York Post,* continue to flourish. Of course, there is also the financial beehive that is Wall Street, which in many ways owes its existence to the poor boy from Nevis.

New York City's most visible monument to Aaron Burr may be JPMorgan Chase; the sprawling financial institution traces its origins back to the Manhattan Company. The corporation's headquarters is located in a skyscraper at 270 Park Avenue. Visitors from around the world stop in to see the two weapons used in the duel, encased in a glass display cabinet. The ornate brass and wood pistols are mounted in such a way that they point directly at each other, inextricably linked yet frozen in eternal opposition. Just like Hamilton and Burr, rivals unto death.

CAST OF CHARACTERS

The Principals

Aaron Burr (1756–1836)
Born into a well-respected New Jersey family. Orphaned by age two. Graduated from Princeton. Elected senator from New York and vice president of the United States. Identified as a Republican, but a political freelancer whose independent streak sowed distrust on both sides. Self-described as a "grave, silent, strange sort of animal." Founded Manhattan Company. Supported rights of immigrants and women. Opposed slavery.

After dueling with Alexander Hamilton in 1804, headed west. Possibly seditious acts led to a celebrated 1807 treason trial. Accused of conspiring to lead an armed insurrection to create a new country. Chief Justice John Marshall threw out the case. Fled to England for four years, then returned. Used his mother's maiden name (Edwards) to elude creditors. Married a wealthy widow in his old age who left him a few months later. Divorce came through on the day he died from a stroke.

Alexander Hamilton (1755–1804)
Born on the Caribbean island of Nevis, "the bastard brat of a Scotch peddler" as John Adams described him. Father abandoned him, and mother died when he was thirteen. Immigrant who made good.

Unstoppable striver. Protégé and aide to General George Washington during the Revolution, known as the "Little Lion." Primary author of *The Federalist Papers,* worked tirelessly to see the Constitution ratified. Treasury secretary under Washington. Considered by some as founder of American capitalism. Prolific writer, thinker—Jefferson called him "a host within himself." Believed in an activist government that promoted commerce and industry.

Achievements so numerous they defy cataloging. Among lesser-known accomplishments: founded BNY Mellon and the *New York Post,* fingered West Point as ideal locale for United States Military Academy.

Supporting Players

John Adams (1735–1826)
Boston lawyer. Led battle in the Continental Congress to declare independence from Britain. Nation's first vice president and second president. Nicknamed "His Rotundity." Brilliant, stubborn, ill tempered. Feuded with fellow Federalist Alexander Hamilton, and frequently derided him in letters to his wife Abigail. Became deeply estranged from Thomas Jefferson, but late in life they renewed their friendship in a series of remarkable letters. Both died on July 4, 1826, fifty years to the day after the signing of the Declaration of Independence.

Theodosia Prevost Burr (1746–1794)
Wife of Aaron Burr. Ten years older than her husband, previously married to British officer who died during Revolutionary War. Spirited, well-read, good intellectual match for Burr. Had five children from her first marriage. Her two sons embraced by Burr as his own, but little is

known of the daughters, most likely raised by relatives. Sickly for much of her second marriage. Her early death devastated Burr.

James Callender (1758–1803)
Scottish-born Republican editor and pamphleteer with a reputation as a scandalmonger. Supported by Thomas Jefferson. Launched vicious attacks against Adams and Hamilton. Later turned on Jefferson by revealing Jefferson's intimate relationship with Sally Hemmings, one of his slaves. Jailed briefly under Alien and Sedition Acts.

Angelica Schuyler Church (1756–1814)
Sister of Alexander Hamilton's wife Eliza; wife of John Barker Church. Beautiful, intelligent, witty. Corresponded frequently with Hamilton. Unsubstantiated rumors of an affair with Hamilton. Made powerful impression on Thomas Jefferson, Benjamin Franklin, and others. Town of Angelica, New York, named after her.

John Barker Church (1748–1818)
Wealthy British-born businessman. Eloped with Angelica Schuyler in 1777, thus becoming Hamilton's brother-in-law. Moved to Europe in 1783: first Paris, then London. Became member of Parliament. Returned to the United States in 1797. Hamilton frequently represented Church in business matters. Involved in creation of the Bank of New York (now BNY Mellon) and the Manhattan Company (now JPMorgan Chase). Fought a duel with Aaron Burr. Owner of the ornate dueling pistols used by Hamilton and Burr in their showdown.

Eliza Hamilton (1757–1854)
Married to Alexander Hamilton. "Best of wives and best of women," Hamilton wrote in one of his final letters. Valued her privacy, burned most of her correspondence. Worked assiduously alongside Hamilton,

aiding him in his prolific writings. Lived fifty years after his death. Devoted herself to defending Hamilton's reputation. Refused to forgive James Monroe for attacking Hamilton's integrity during the Reynolds affair. Founded the first private orphanage in New York City, in memory of her husband, the orphan child who made good. Never remarried.

Philip Hamilton (1782–1801)
Eldest son of Alexander and Eliza Hamilton. Graduated from Columbia College. Intellect comparable to his father's. Killed in 1801 duel with George Eacker at Weehawken, New Jersey. Used pistols employed in Hamilton-Burr duel three years later on the same spot.

John Jay (1745–1829)
America's forgotten founder. President of the Continental Congress, secretary of foreign affairs, chief justice of the Supreme Court, and governor of New York. Coauthor of *The Federalist Papers*. Negotiated 1783 Treaty of Paris, which concluded the American Revolution, and the 1794 Jay Treaty, which earned him much vitriol.

Thomas Jefferson (1743–1826)
Principal author of the Declaration of Independence. Third president of the United States, governor of Virginia, secretary of state, and vice president. Known as the "Sage of Monticello." Among founders of the Democrat-Republican party (aka the Republican party, but different from the current Republican party). Powerful defender of individual rights, declared "all men are created equal," yet owned slaves and fathered children with his slave, Sally Hemmings. Ordered Aaron Burr arrested in 1807 on charges of treason, which ultimately were dismissed.

Charles Lee (1732–1782)

Unsavory American Revolutionary War general. Former British officer. Captured by the British in 1776. May have conspired with them, before being released back to the Americans. Became George Washington's second-in-command, but not-so-secretly thought he himself should be in charge. Court-martialed for treachery at the Battle of Monmouth. Stricken by fever and died at age fifty.

James Madison (1751–1836)

Brilliant political theorist from Virginia. The "Father of the Constitution." Secretary of state under Jefferson. Succeeded him as president. Small in stature, shy in public, nicknamed "Little Jemmy." Worked with Hamilton to bring about the Constitutional Convention. Coauthored *The Federalist Papers*. Opposed Hamilton's financial plans in the House and became a strong ally of Thomas Jefferson. Introduced to wife Dolly by Aaron Burr. President during the War of 1812, when the White House was burned.

James Monroe (1758–1831)

Fifth president of the United States. Republican ally of Jefferson and Madison. Hamilton suspected him of leaking damaging documents, which nearly led to a duel between them. As president, established the Monroe Doctrine to keep the Americas free of European intervention. Late in life, known as the "Last of the Cocked Hats" because he wore a tricorn hat long after they went out of style.

Maria Reynolds (1768–1832)

Conniving blond bombshell. Married at age fifteen. Conspired with husband James Reynolds to seduce and blackmail Hamilton. Divorced Reynolds, married his partner in crime, Jacob Clingman.

Still later, married a Philadelphia doctor. Found religion. Became a pillar of her community.

Philip Schuyler (1733–1804)
Father of Eliza Hamilton and Angelica Schuyler Church. Revolutionary War general. Major landowner and powerful political figure in New York. Served as a United States senator until defeated by Aaron Burr in 1791. Died only four months after Hamilton.

George Washington (1732–1799)
The "Father of Our Country." Commanding general of the Continental Army, president of the Continental Congress, first president of the United States. A Virginia planter whose military experiences in the French and Indian War led him to be chosen commander of the nascent American Army in 1775. Masked his temper under a stoic demeanor. Alexander Hamilton's mentor and political patron; the two men trusted and depended on each other. Washington owned hundreds of slaves whom he freed upon his death.

Minor Characters

Theodosia Burr Alston (1783–1813)
Daughter of Aaron Burr. Also his confidante and adviser. Married James Alston, who became governor of South Carolina during the War of 1812. Lost at sea in 1813 aboard the schooner *Patriot* on the way to see her father after his return from England.

James Bayard (1767–1815)
Federalist congressman from Delaware. Played a pivotal role in the presidential election of 1800.

Aedanus Burke (1743–1802)

Irish-born lawyer who, as a South Carolina congressman, nearly fought a duel with Alexander Hamilton. Aaron Burr's second in his duel with John Barker Church. Later became chief justice of the South Carolina Supreme Court.

James Cheetham (1772–1810)

Editor and publisher of the *American Citizen.* Launched fierce attacks on Aaron Burr and others that led to frequent libel suits. The newspaper ceased publication after his death.

George Clinton (1739–1812)

Longtime Republican governor of New York. Rival and ally of Aaron Burr. Enemy of Hamilton. Elected vice president in 1804 after Jefferson dumped Burr.

William Coleman (1766–1829)

Massachusetts-born lawyer and journalist. Editor of the *New York Evening Post* for twenty-eight years. Compiled and published accounts of the Hamilton-Burr duel in 1804. After dying of a stroke, he was succeeded by the legendary editor, abolitionist, and poet William Cullen Bryant.

Matthew Livingston Davis (1773–1850)

New York politician, journalist, businessman. Friend and admirer of Aaron Burr. Burr's first biographer. Not only had access to Burr's papers, but also had many conversations with Burr about events in his life.

George Eacker (1774–1804)

New York lawyer who killed Philip Hamilton in a duel. Republican who had attacked Alexander Hamilton in a speech. Died three years later of consumption, now known as tuberculosis.

Albert Gallatin (1761–1849)
Swiss-born politician and statesman. Ejected from Senate by Federalists for being foreign-born. Came back to Washington as a Pennsylvania congressman. Longtime secretary of the treasury under Thomas Jefferson and James Madison.

Nathanael Greene (1742–1786)
Revolutionary War general under George Washington. Rhode Island–born Quaker turned military man. Rose from the rank of private to become Washington's most trusted general. His troops forced General Cornwallis to abandon the Carolinas, leading to the British defeat at the Battle of Yorktown.

Robert Goodloe Harper (1765–1825)
Federalist congressman from South Carolina. Remembered for the phrase "Millions for defense, but not one cent for tribute." Later a senator from Maryland. Launched an unsuccessful campaign for vice president in 1816.

Marquis de Lafayette (1757–1834)
French general who aided Washington and befriended Hamilton. Survived the French Revolution and received a hero's welcome when he returned to the United States in 1824.

John Lansing (1754–1829)
Simultaneously mayor of Albany and New York delegate to the Constitutional Convention. Left convention in anger with fellow delegate Robert Yates. Refused to sign the Constitution. Fought ratification. Later became chief justice of the New York Supreme Court. In 1829, left a Manhattan hotel to mail a letter and was never seen again.

John Laurens (1754–1782)

Wealthy scion of a South Carolina family, who befriended Hamilton when they both served on Washington's staff. Briefly served as minister to France. Opposed to slavery. Led a failed effort to form a three-thousand-man African American regiment. Killed in one of the final battles of the Revolution.

Robert Livingston (1746–1813)

Head of a powerful New York family. Chancellor of New York, the highest judicial post in the state (it no longer exists). With Jefferson, Franklin, and Adams, sat on the committee that drafted the Declaration of Independence. Broke with Hamilton to join the Republicans. Later served as Jefferson's minister to France. Negotiated the Louisiana Purchase.

Alexander McDougall (1732–1786)

New York merchant, turned patriotic activist, turned Revolutionary War general. Commissioned Alexander Hamilton as an officer and later commanded Aaron Burr. First president of the Bank of New York, founded by Hamilton.

Gouverneur Morris (1752–1816)

One of the signers of the Constitution. Credited with writing the preamble and fashioning much of the language of the document. Federalist ally and friend of Hamilton. Became a United States senator from New York. First name rhymes with "rocketeer."

Robert Morris Jr. (1734–1806)

Liverpool-born merchant, privateer, and speculator. Apprenticed in the Philadelphia shipping trade. Helped finance the American Revolution. Signer of the Declaration of Independence. Went bankrupt in the panic of 1796. Served time in debtors' prison.

Frederick Muhlenberg (1750–1801)
Republican congressman from Pennsylvania. Served as the first and third speaker of the house. Minister in the Lutheran Church. Figured in the Reynolds affair.

Matthias Ogden (1754–1791)
Aaron Burr's childhood friend. Fought with Burr at the Battle of Quebec. Promoted to lieutenant colonel, served at Monmouth and Yorktown. Later became a wealthy lawyer, established a stagecoach line, and built a tannery and mint. His life was cut short by yellow fever at age thirty-six.

Nathaniel Pendleton (1756–1821)
Southern lawyer and federal judge in Georgia and later New York State. Served as Alexander Hamilton's second for his duel with Aaron Burr.

Charles Cotesworth Pinckney (1746–1825)
Member of a prominent South Carolina family. Delegate to the Constitutional Convention. Became a leading Federalist. One of the American ministers in France who stood fast during the XYZ Affair. Federalist candidate for vice president in 1800. Ran for president in 1804 and 1808. A three-time loser. Not to be confused with his brother, Thomas Pinckney, who ran for vice president in 1796. And lost.

Robert Troup (1756–1832)
Hamilton's roommate at King's College. An aide to General Horatio Gates during the Battle of Saratoga. Became a Federalist lawyer and judge in New York City. Knew both Burr and Hamilton well.

William Van Ness (1778–1826)
New York lawyer who eventually became a United States federal judge. Burr's close friend and second at his duel with Hamilton. One

of his brothers became mayor of Washington, D.C.; another was governor of Vermont.

Noah Webster (1758–1843)
Erudite Federalist advocate and newspaper editor. "Father of American Scholarship and Education." Compiler of *Webster's Dictionary.*

Levi Weeks (1776–1819)
A young carpenter charged with murder. Defended by Burr and Hamilton, among others. Became a well-respected architect and builder in Natchez, Mississippi.

James Wilkinson (1757–1825)
Notorious American general. A spy for Spain. Slippery scoundrel who survived three courts-martial as he rose to commander of the United States Army. Allegedly conspired with Burr to sever territory from the United States and establish an independent country. Turned on Burr to save his own skin.

Oliver Wolcott Jr. (1760–1833)
Succeeded Alexander Hamilton as secretary of the treasury. Federalist who opposed President Adams's efforts to end the "Quasi War." Resigned from Adams's cabinet. Later became governor of Connecticut.

Robert Yates (1738–1801)
Anti-Federalist delegate to the Constitutional Convention. Left early. Refused to sign. Opposed ratification. Both Hamilton and Burr supported him in a failed 1789 race for governor. In a striking coincidence, Yates later became chief justice of the New York Supreme Court—just like fellow Constitution refusenik John Lansing.

ACKNOWLEDGMENTS

This book represents a joyous reunion with the editor who launched my *Greatest Stories Never Told* series, Mauro Dipreta, now vice president and publisher of Hachette Books. He contacted me in the early days of the Hamilton mania whipped up by Lin-Manuel Miranda and his Broadway show, and asked if I would be interested in writing about the rivalry, squeezing the whole story into a compact and accessible volume. I jumped at the chance. I have long been fascinated by the conflict between Hamilton and Burr, devouring many books about it. The chance to write my own take on this amazing tale was something too good to be missed. I'm incredibly grateful to Mauro and the whole team at Hachette, including Associate Managing Editor Mike Olivo, copy editor Diana Drew, Michelle Aielli, Betsy Hulsebosch, Mark Harrington, and David Lamb. Together they helped create a far more polished product than I ever could have on my own.

I want to thank my own team as well. First, the good souls in the Lexington Peets Pals who acted as both a sounding board and support group during the time I was writing the book. My sister Cathy Hurst and my history-fiend friend Robert Paratore both read the manuscript before it was submitted and offered valuable suggestions and reassurances (always important!). Doug Hamilton, a fifth-generation grandson of Alexander, was kind enough to spend hours of his own time researching the answers to questions I asked about the dinner at Fraunces Tavern one week before the duel, the opening scene of the book.

Finally, in a class by herself, is my wife, Marilyn Rea Beyer. She has been the unsung collaborator on every book I've written, every documentary I've produced, offering valuable feedback, helping to shape tricky passages, reading every word with painstaking care, and always offering unstinting support. This project was especially dear to her heart, since she shares a birthday with Alexander Hamilton, and has been captivated by the story since she first wrote a book report about him in fifth grade. Marilyn and I have been a team for more than thirty years, and my life has been the better for it in every way imaginable. Thank you.

SELECTED SOURCES

I gratefully acknowledge the many fine authors and historians whose work I consulted in writing this book. Here are the sources I relied upon the most.

Online:

Founders Online: http://founders.archives.gov

The National Archives created this online treasure trove of primary source material: a searchable archive with more than 175,000 pieces of correspondence and other writings from the Founding Fathers, including more than 7,000 documents emanating from the pen of Alexander Hamilton.

The Diary of Elizabeth De Hart Bleecker: https://www.nypl.org/blog/2016/01/14/dehardt-bleecker-diary

Detail makes a story come alive, and the diary of this young woman in New York City during the 1800s yielded some wonderful tidbits, including weather on the days leading up to Hamilton's death.

Books

Bowen, Catherine Drinker. *Miracle at Philadelphia: The Story of the Constitutional Convention, May to September, 1787.* Boston: Little, Brown and Company, 1966.

Burrows, Edwin G., and Mike Wallace. *Gotham: A History of New York City to 1898*. New York: Oxford University Press, 1999.

Chernow, Ron. *Alexander Hamilton*. New York: Penguin Books, 2005.

Coleman, William. *A Collection of the Facts and Documents, Relative to the Death of Major General Alexander Hamilton*. New York: Printed by Hopkins and Seymour for I. Riley and Co. Booksellers, 1804.

Ellis, Joseph. *Founding Brothers*. New York: Alfred A. Knopf, 2001.

Ferling, John. *Adams vs. Jefferson: The Tumultuous Election of 1800*. New York: Oxford University Press, 2004.

Fleming, Thomas. *Duel: Alexander Hamilton, Aaron Burr and the Future of America*. New York: Basic Books, 2000.

Hamilton, James. *Reminiscences of James A. Hamilton, or, Men and Events at Home and Abroad During Three Quarters of a Century*. New York: Charles Scribner and Co., 1869.

Isenberg, Nancy. *Fallen Founder: The Life of Aaron Burr*. Boston: Penguin Books, 2007.

Kline, Mary Jo, ed. *Political Correspondence and Public Papers of Aaron Burr*. Princeton, NJ: Princeton University Press, 1983.

Langguth, A. J. *Patriots: The Men Who Started the American Revolution*. New York: Simon & Schuster, 1988.

Lomask, Milton. *Aaron Burr: The Years from Princeton to Vice President, 1765–1805*. New York: Farrar, Straus and Giroux, 1979.

McCullough, David. *John Adams*. New York: Simon & Schuster, 2001.

INDEX